Mrs. Sunday's Problem

MRS. SUNDAY'S PROBLEM

and other stories

Harold Fickett

Fleming H. Revell Company
Old Tappan, New Jersey

Scripture quotation is from the King James Version of the Bible.

Library of Congress Cataloging in Publication Data

Fickett, Harold L
  Mrs. Sunday's problem, and other stories.

  CONTENTS: A sycamore tree.—Christbirth.—The
missionary conference.—Persecuted for Christ's sake.
—Palm Sunday.—Mrs. Sunday's problem.
  1. Christian fiction.   I. Title.
PZ4.F449Mi [PS3556.I33] 813'.5'4 78-31469
ISBN 0-8007-0996-9'

TO my father and mother.

Contents

Introduction: Why Fiction?

THE PRACTICAL PERSON often does not like fiction. He finds life difficult, and when he reads, he wants help; he wants advice on his marital problems or counsel about his career. If he is a Christian, he wants to know how he can improve his spiritual life. He is looking for answers. With all the books he has to choose from, expressing so many different points of view, he tries to choose those which are written by reliable authorities.

Picking up a book of fiction, the practical person is suspicious. He has unpleasant memories of English classes in which the story or novel he had read—parts of which he enjoyed, parts of which bored him—turned out to be something quite other than he had expected. It seemed that reading was a kind of occult activity for the initiated who could detect allusions and symbols, for those who could see that a story about a man and a woman was really about a nineteenth-century philosophy. And so, picking up a book of fiction, the practical person hesitates: why should he trouble himself? why can't the fiction writer say what he means? how can he trust the writer's credentials?

9

The practical person does not realize that he can read all the books by acknowledged authorities on psychology and religion and still not have any idea how that material applies to his life. Even if an author tells us exactly what to do in a given situation, the situation will soon become so complex that it will bear little relation to that which preceded it. Each of us needs to understand how principles and ethical dictums can be incorporated in his actions. Moreover and more fundamentally, we need the "eyes to see" how religious perceptions of life are inherent and present in our own lives. God is love. But what does the love of God mean when I am suffering?

Stories try to answer that question and others like it. In fiction the author tries to take on the whole of life, not one area of knowledge. He tries to reveal a vision of life as it is lived; to speak about life through the way that we come to know it—actions and feelings. Fiction is not life, though, and it is not autobiography. Figuratively, it is a language, with its own grammar of images and logic of plot, which allows it to speak the truth about life in a way ordinary language cannot. If we cannot see how ethical concerns are present in a story, there is a good chance that we will be blind to those concerns when they appear in life; for they appear to us in life as they do in stories, veiled in circumstances and embodied in other people.

Most people, even if they do not like fiction, have an intuitive sense of story logic; they have to, in order to understand the meaning of their own lives. For what are we trying to make of our lives but stories? The story begins at birth, develops during years of education, begins again in earnest with work and family, climaxes with the achievements of middle life, and finds its denouement in old age. It is nothing but a story, and it is everything.

The Scriptures consist largely of stories: Old Testament narratives about the Jews and their patriarchs, and the Gospels, which are essentially biographies. The form in which religious truth is presented to us is in accord with our own ways of experiencing and understanding. It remains alive for us, as all good stories remain alive, because it is preserved in authentic detail. The fiction writer can see himself as working within the tradition of biblical narrative, although he cannot claim divine inspiration. His task is simply to rework the old and ever-true story into new stories which take into account the present circumstances. His credentials consist solely in how well he does this.

I have tried in the short stories that follow to capture moments in which grace is granted to members of one fictional Baptist congregation. The appearance of grace allows the protagonists of the stories to move toward God, to love Him. It does not force them to love God, however. There is always the possibility that they will reject God's grace and turn away from Him. No one should be surprised that some do turn away. The appearance of grace is not a benign event. It is charged with terror, for it demands a price—everything—the complete sacrifice and immolation of our natural being in order that we may become supernatural creatures.

The basis of art is truth, both in matter and in mode. The person who aims after art in his work aims after truth, in an imaginative sense, no more and no less.

Flannery O'Connor

Here is the church
Here is the steeple
Open the doors
And see all the people.

Children's rhyme

Observe that for the novelist who has remained Christian, like myself, man is someone creating himself or destroying himself . . . . The human being as I conceive him in the novel is a being caught up in the drama of salvation, even if he doesn't know it.

Francois Mauriac

A Sycamore Tree

AFTER SERVING FOR THREE YEARS as an usher, Allen Gresham was elected head usher of the First Baptist Church of San Cariño. As head usher it was his job to make certain that each week there would be enough ushers—at least a half dozen beside himself—to distribute the weekly bulletin, seat the congregation, and take the offering. He also directed his troops in the event that anything untoward happened: occasionally, someone stood up in the middle of the sermon and declared that the preacher was Antichrist or prophesied the destruction of the Santa Ana Freeway in an earthquake, and the disturbance had to be removed. It was also Allen's job, after the morning worship service had ended, to total the amount of the offering and keep the church's books up-to-date.

The first Sunday Allen assumed his new duties, he took the head usher's post, standing at the very back of the church's sanctuary in the right aisle. Except at the beginning of the service, when he seated people, and during the offering, it was not necessary for him to stand; he might have taken a seat on the aisle like all the other ushers. But Allen Gresham was a short man, not quite five feet one inch.

He was boyishly handsome; at thirty-five, wearing a

15

subtle plaid sports jacket and worsted slacks, he had the look of a favorite son. His thick, shining brown hair swept across his high forehead, his complexion was clear and smooth; indeed, his slight double chin seemed lingering baby fat. Only the surprising breadth of his forehead and his rather owlish eyes hinted at dwarfness. But basically, he appeared a quite normal, short man.

Before he had become an usher, he had come to church every Sunday, hoping to find a seat on the aisle or behind a child, and invariably there were no aisle seats available or, once he had settled himself behind a diminutive eight-year-old, the child decided he wanted to sit between Mommy and Daddy, and so Mommy moved over and the woman's teased hairdo blanked out Allen's view of the preacher. And so on this Sunday, when he assumed the position of head usher, he let himself stand at the back. He smiled affably, glancing about to see if anyone thought his standing there peculiar, but when his glance was returned, so was his affable smile. The red carnation in his lapel, which signified that he was the head usher, dressed him in unquestioned authority.

Reverend March preached on Zacchaeus that Sunday, and Allen saw every moment of the pastor's twenty-five minute, gesticulating performance. The sermon moved Allen. He had always believed the Gospel and affirmed the truth of Protestant doctrine, but he had wondered whether or not he actually felt any love for God or had known divine love. As Reverend March described Zacchaeus, however, picturing Zacchaeus scrambling up into the sycamore tree to see Jesus pass by, Allen identified with Zacchaeus. His position as head usher was his sycamore tree, and now he was standing in the aisle to see Jesus through Reverend March's preaching. Allen felt that Jesus recognized his gesture as He had recognized Zacchaeus. For once, Christ's words were meant especially for Allen, and his communion with Christ was as real as the meal Jesus and Zacchaeus had shared. While Reverend March gave the invitation to accept Christ as Saviour and Lord, Allen stepped into the foyer and dabbed his owlish eyes with his monogrammed handkerchief.

Two weeks after Allen became head usher, on a Thursday, Allen and his wife, Stasia, sat in the cathedral-ceilinged living room of their home. Stasia was at one end of the room, writing letters at a very good reproduction of a *Louis Quinze* desk. Allen was at the other end of the room, sitting in the middle of the wraparound couch before the fireplace, glancing through a brochure about a new line of washers and dryers which he was considering selling out of his white-goods store.

It was six o'clock, an hour Allen often enjoyed, relaxing in the atmosphere of the ample life which he had provided for his family. He heard the delighted screams of his two daughters, Gail and Barbara; they were jumping on the trampoline in the backyard. He could see them through the window from where he sat, their figures indistinct in the lingering light of the spring day; steamy vapors rose off the heated pool behind them.

He looked at his wife and thought her lovely. Stasia was of Hungarian descent. She was small-boned, petite; her face was beautiful and doll-like. Bent over, her black hair falling about her face from the part at her widow's peak, framing her almost violet eyes, she held her pen tightly in her thin, aristocratic fingers. Allen loved her extravagantly.

"Allen," she said, noticing that he was looking at her, "have you seen this?" She held up an envelope which, by its address window, Allen could tell was a bill. "It's from the decorator who did the guest room."

"Leave it there, and I'll take it to the office tomorrow," Allen said. "I'm sure I told that woman I wanted the bill sent to my office."

"She says she's sent two notices to your office already, Allen."

"Must have overlooked them. There's so many to overlook since we bought the house, you know." Allen laughed, a sort of breathless chuckle.

"You're sure it was just overlooked?" Stasia asked, and her tone implied that this oversight might be more revealing of the true state of their finances than Allen cared to admit.

"Honey," Allen said, "I'll pay it right now, if you like. I brought the checkbook home with me." Allen crossed the living room and picked up the bill. He wrote out a check for three hundred and fourteen dollars and thirty-six cents and handed it to Stasia. Then he went back and sat on the couch and deducted the amount of the check from his balance. He was already overdrawn at the bank by some six hundred dollars, and this check to the decorator brought the figure to nearly a thousand. His checking account was the type that allowed for overdrafts, but only up to five hundred dollars. He would have to make a few sales the next morning and rush the money to the bank, so that it would be there Monday or

Tuesday morning when the checks arrived.

Business was slow Friday and nonexistent Saturday. In the late afternoon on Saturday, Allen deposited what money he had taken in the last two days, using the bank's computerized deposit machine. But he was still almost one hundred dollars short of maintaining his balance within the allowable imbalance. He returned to the store, told his salesman, David Bell, to go home, locked up, and sat in his office at the back of the store, wondering what he should do. He determined that he would have to call the decorator Monday and ask her to delay cashing the check.

Through his office window he looked out onto the floor of his store, toward the glass windows at the front, and the cash register there, back again to the stolid major appliances. He viewed it as an extension of himself; he saw in it the history of his business career, the aggregate and sum of his life. He knew that ever since he had purchased his family's new home about one year ago, business had been poor and his finances critically overextended. He would have been all right if he had not thrown all of his capital and the money he could borrow into several speculative investments, desert land that would take years to increase in value, a medical building which was still half-unoccupied, and the only nonprofitable fast-food franchise in Southern California. Each month he juggled payments, keeping more and more of his bills in the air. And now this decorator's bill had fallen in such a casual yet portentous way that he was afraid. Unless business improved, he might lose the store; and if he did, it would be somehow as if time itself had deserted him.

On Sunday at the morning worship service, Allen stood in the aisle with the felt-lined offering plate in his hand. Reverend March ended his prefatory comments to the offertory prayer with a joking remark: He said that the peoples' offering acknowledged that all good things came from God, that giving was a way of testifying to the fact that God had met one's needs. But, of course—he added flippantly—if God hadn't met one's needs, perhaps one should take something out of the offering. Then he prayed.

Allen passed the plate from one aisle to the next. Reverend March's little joke struck him as distinctly unfunny. As he watched the soiled dollar bills and offering envelopes slightly larger than the size of a once-folded check accumulate, the joke became more and more sour. Allen noticed that the people did not appear thankful. He had often seen the prim, set expressions that the members of the congregation wore after depositing their offerings and noticed their hurried manner, but until that day he had never seen what their manner signified. They were relieved, not grateful; they clearly wanted to divest themselves of this unpleasant responsibility and get on with the service. He thought what hypocrites they were. He also thought that Reverend March should control his tongue.

Allen remained angry and disconsolate throughout the service. He found Reverend March's sermon uninspired. He left the sanctuary during the altar call to take the day's offering from the usher's anteroom to the business office on the first floor of the education building. There in a small, cramped room, painted an institutional green, with filing cabinets lining the walls, he sat to count the money at a gray metal desk. A lone poster graced the

walls; it hung above the desk and pictured a childishly painted sun with the words "God Loves You" scrawled underneath.

From the desk drawer Allen extracted two black notebooks and a blue covered ledger. He went through the envelopes, entering the amount given that week by each member in one of the black notebooks where the record was kept as to how well each member fulfilled his pledge commitment, and then, if the envelope contained a check, he entered the amount in the blue ledger. He totaled the checks on the church's old-fashioned adding machine and then began to separate the cash into like denominations. He came upon a curiosity; a fresh, newly minted, Benjamin Franklin bearing, one-hundred-dollar bill. Occasionally someone put a fifty-dollar bill into one of the envelopes, but he had never seen a one-hundred-dollar bill which had been tossed into the plate.

He finished sorting the cash. Once he had counted all the loose cash, he could see that the total from the checks and cash equalled a normal Sunday's offering without the inclusion of the one-hundred-dollar bill. He picked up the magic bill, stretching it between the pinching fingers of his two hands. He could feel the minute relief, the uneven texture of the engraving which bordered the bill.

The presence of this bill on this day when he needed money so much seemed to him miraculous. Reverend March had been joking about taking from the offering, but perhaps he had been led to make that remark. The church would not miss the money. He looked up, a man looking to heaven for a sign. He focused on the poster: "God Loves You."

He still held the bill between his two hands, but had drawn it closer to his body, his shoulders hunched over, guarding the bill against another's sight. But he was alone in the room. He looked about and behind him to assure himself of this fact, and saw only the ring of filing cabinets (though these cabinets seemed somehow less inanimate, had become presences, their square labels so many Cyclopean eyes). Then he remembered the story about Jesus telling Peter to pay the government's tribute with a coin he would find in the mouth of a fish. The story came to him so suddenly, he thought it must be an inspiration. He took his flat leather wallet from his coat's breast pocket and slipped the bill next to the lone five there, across from the shingled row of credit cards.

Then he totaled the offering, entered the amount in the other black notebook, and began binding the checks and the various denominations of cash with rubber bands. He slipped all the money down the long throat of a bank bag and rolled his chair over to the spot in the linoleum floor where a loose tile covered the floor safe. He left the money in the safe and locked the office on his way out.

On Monday morning he deposited the one-hundred-dollar bill in his checking account. Driving from the bank to the store, he felt at peace concerning the affair. He had always given his fair share to the church. In return, God had blessed his business. The economy had generally taken a turn for the worse; it was natural that his business should go through a slow period, though not quite as slow as last week had been. In His providence, God had seen fit to grant a special grace to Allen. He felt

humbled by this and resolved to make a special contri-
bution to the church once he was out of the financial
woods. God was on his side: business could do nothing
but improve.

Allen's business did improve that next week and the
fortnight thereafter until the end of the month. But after
Allen had paid the bills that demanded immediate attention, a notice that he owed another month's rent on his
store came, along with a threatening letter informing
him that he was already three months behind in his
payments. He put the bill aside for two Sundays, sold
washers and dryers, and took enough money from the
church's funds to insure that he would not lose the store.
This time, unless he paid the money back, there was no
question as to whether or not he was stealing.

Almost daily he prayed and promised God that he
would repay the money. In order to demonstrate the au-
thenticity of his intentions, he went into his closet—as
it said to do in his King James Bible—and there, among
his rows of oxblood and black business shoes and
the nutty odor of old socks, he knelt and mumbled his
vows.

During the next six months business continued to be
poor. Allen was forced to sell his new home and move
his family into a tacky apartment building called the
Northern Lights. (The ceiling of their three-bedroom
apartment was flecked with mica, so that it sparkled in
the dark.) He also sold his luxury cars and bought two
Plymouths. His financial situation greatly improved.
Even though Allen had owned his home for only a year,

due to inflation, he had been able to sell it for a tremendous profit and apply that money to his debts. Unfortunately, the sale of his home did not completely solve Allen's financial problems. He always seemed short of petty cash. Embezzling from the church's funds became one of Allen's regular sources of income. He never took much, only what he needed to tide him over.

To Allen's surprise, Stasia adapted very well to their new living arrangements. In their house she had always seemed unsure of herself, constantly asking Allen about trivial household matters. In their apartment she organized their cramped quarters with a certain genius and became a little more forceful in disciplining the girls. She loved preparing thrifty meals. For dinner one night she served an indigestible Hungarian blood sausage. After Allen stopped wondering where in their homogenized neighborhood she could have found such a thing, he realized that his Stasia, whom he had always treated as a frail aristocrat, had the instincts of the stockiest plough horse of a Hungarian peasant.

As part of his program to improve his finances, Allen let his assistant, David Bell, go. Allen decided that personal service had made his store a success and would reestablish it as such; the customer must know that he was buying from a man whose livelihood depended upon his reputation. Besides, Allen knew himself to be a crackerjack salesman.

The ability to recognize instantly what type of person the customer wanted to deal with, plus the ability to play that part, made Allen a good salesman. When he returned to selling full time, he found that he still had the ability to recognize the role required, but his timing had deteriorated badly. He thought that his timing would come back to him; it did not, it degenerated.

One day a matronly woman walked into the store. He knew instantly that she wanted him to be her bright son, to impress her with his grasp of the complexities of the machinery, to assure her that he knew exactly what she needed, and to unburden her of this worrisome matter. She was writing out the check when Allen made a remark about her generosity (the washer and dryer were to be a present for the woman's daughter, who was about to give birth). The woman flushed and said that if the machines were that expensive, her son-in-law would never accept them. Allen nodded his head and ushered the woman out the door. His demeanor remained kind, but his eyes were vacant—a man aware of his own death in the midst of the humdrum world.

Allen felt cursed. He felt that in some invisible way God had marked him as He had marked Cain, so that the world, although unaware of the exact nature of his sin, knew Allen to be an outcast. Repaying the church's money became an exigency; he knew he would not regain his timing until he had done so.

He spent the next afternoon in his deserted store, thinking about where he might borrow the money. Banks were out of the question—they would take one look at his finances and show him the door. His friends were church members; he did not want to go to them. Not because they might suspect him of any wrongdoing, but because he was so distraught that he might break down and confess.

He finally called Richard Hughes, a friend from high school and a C.P.A. through whose advice he had made a few small but rewarding investments.

Richard came on the line and they exchanged hellos.

"I haven't seen you at Rotary lately, Allen," Richard said. "How is everything, Amigo? How's Stasia and the girls?"

"They're fine, doing real well."

"We heard you moved out of your house in Pleasant Estates. Didn't it suit you?"

Allen had not even asked for the loan yet, and already Richard had begun exacting a usurious interest. One forgot about "old friends," and then remembered too late. But he was desperate enough to play the groveling suppliant, so he said, "To be frank, Dick (he knew Richard did not like to be called Dick), my store's been hit by the recession. I've had to cut back. The new place was too much, with the economy as it is now."

"Know what you mean."

"That's partly the reason I called. I need a loan, Richard."

"Amigo, I can't. I'm really sorry. I've got all my capital tied up in a futures deal. But listen, you might be interested. The Chicago Mercantile Exchange is offering futures on frozen pork bellies. The price is bound to rise. A lot of the farmers can't afford to feed their stock until marketing time—the fuel costs have driven up the cost of feeding their stock something like six hundred percent. They need capital, that's why they're selling these futures at bargain-basement prices."

"How many hogs do you own?"

"You don't understand. Didn't I ever tell you about futures? I don't own any pork bellies, but by paying one and one-half percent of the total value of the bellies, I'm entitled to buy fifty thousand of them at the price which the future specifies."

"You can come up with that kind of money?"

"Allen, I don't *have* to come up with the money to actually buy the pork bellies. I merely exercise my option to take possession of the bellies once they're ready for market, then I turn around and sell them for a higher price. It's paperwork at this end, but the money is very real at the other."

"I think I understand."

"Listen, Allen, if you really need some money, why don't you come into this deal with me? I can let you in for two thousand. You could make twenty, thirty thousand dollars."

"Richard, I've just asked for a loan. Would I do that if I had money lying around to invest?"

"Sell something, Amigo; a car, an heirloom. I'm telling you, Allen, this deal could get you well again. Don't you own some desert property?"

The man had an elephantine memory when it came to money. "Yes," Allen said, "I do, though it's not worth much now. But say I *can* get the money somehow, what's the horizon time on the investment?"

"Nine months. The hogs take their time fattening up."

"Richard, this is crazy."

"I've never given you a bad tip, Amigo. Have I?"

"How soon do I have to get you the money?"

"Within two weeks. One more thing. The investment's solid—I wouldn't tell you to sell the family jewels if it wasn't—but it *is* pure speculation. If we aren't going to make a profit, we simply don't exercise the option."

"Meaning?"

"Write it off your taxes. The money's gone. All of it."

"Let me call you back."

"Sure, Allen. Waiting to hear from you. Say hello to Stasia and the girls for me."

Though it was risky, the idea of such an investment appealed to Allen. A chance to get even, that's what he wanted. He spent the next few days exhausting possible sources. He called the real estate agent who handled his desert property and found that though he had put twenty thousand into the land, he could not sell the property now for two thousand dollars. He could not sell it at any price, in fact—no one wanted to purchase land that would sell that cheaply. The agent said that there was a bill pending before the state legislature which would bring water to the area. If Allen would wait a little longer, they might be able to sell the land as farm acreage. Allen said, "Fine, fine," and hung up.

Allen thought about selling Stasia's car, but then he would have to explain to her what he was doing. Once he had admitted their difficulties to her, she began to quiz him almost nightly as to the state of their affairs. Very quickly, she became shrewd; he could no longer misrepresent the smallest details. Her peasant instincts would never approve of a purely speculative venture, especially one that would take her car away from her. Their relationship had changed: He had forfeited the right to be the little god of their household, conferring upon his family the benefits of his inscrutable ways.

That next Sunday, Allen sat in the business office, totaling the offering. It took him longer than usual. As they

did once a month, the church had celebrated communion. On communion Sundays, the church took a special
offering for the poor, called the deacon's fund. After he
had totaled the regular offering, he licked his thumb and
counted through the pile of one dollar bills given to the
deacon's fund. He entered the amount collected for the
deacon's fund in one of the black notebooks. He saw that
it had been a long time since the deacons had used their
fund to help the poor—long enough for five thousand
dollars to collect in the account.

The figure inspired a physical sense of desperation in
Allen; it felt as if something solid in his chest broke
apart. He may have blacked out for a moment, for he
found himself with his head resting on the pillow of his
overlapping hands. He did not remember assuming this
position, and he had the abrupt and eerie sense of reen-
tering the world, as if he had suddenly awakened in the
night. Money: The thought returned with the immediacy
of a scent, the stinging odor of a sawdust mill.

Allen was not unaware of the irony that a fund for the
poor should hold the money he needed to become rich
once again. He could not steal from this fund even if he
wanted to, because only the head deacon, a Lincoln-
esque figure with a forthright, dull mind, and the pastor
were empowered to administer the funds. He was not
poor enough to ask to be helped, though he would become poor if he did not regain his touch as a salesman,
and that seemed contingent upon paying the church
back. But still, he thought, it could not hurt to ask. He
would not lie (although he would not say anything about
the investment), he would simply ask Reverend March
for a loan. The thought gave him hope, the feeling that

the world might once more become comfortably inhabit-
able.

Allen knew that Reverend March took Monday off, so
he waited until the evening to call him. As the phone
rang, he practiced saying his name a few times, but when
the pastor answered, Allen's voice began at a high pitch
and then fell, so that the sound was garbled.

"Who?" Reverend March asked.

"Allen Gresham."

"Yes, Allen. Just a minute." He heard Reverend March
tell his young son Benjamin to turn down the TV set.
There was the scrambled sound of a phone being picked
up again, and Reverend March was back on the line. "Go
ahead. What's on your mind?"

"We're in some trouble, Pastor."

"No one's ill," the pastor said declaratively. "I saw the
whole family Sunday, didn't I?"

"Financial trouble. The recession."

"Well, I was going to speak with you. Our dishwasher
spots the glasses horrendously. What if I came in and
talked to you about it?"

"Well fine, but what I wanted to ask is whether or not
there might be some ready money available. I'm behind
in the rent, Pastor, and I'm about to lose the store. If I
could just have a loan—perhaps from the deacon's fund.
People will start spending again—they're a little afraid
right now."

"You need how much?"

"Two thousand."

"What if I contacted some of the men in the church?"

"Pastor, I'd really rather not have people know. It might be bad for business."

"The church doesn't loan money, Allen. I doubt there is even that much in the deacon's fund."

"The deacon's fund has five thousand dollars in it."

There was a pause. "You keep those books. I forgot," Reverend March said. Another silence, then he said, his voice sharp with agitation, "We might as well be bankers."

"What?"

"The deacons, Allen. They gall me sometimes. But about your problem: If the money is there, let's go ahead and put it to some use. Two thousand will suffice?"

"Yes, yes, I know it's a lot. I'm grateful, Pastor. I felt so desperate."

"Five thousand dollars," the pastor said. "How can the deacons justify that kind of money sitting idle in a fund for the poor when the area's in a recession? You've started me thinking, Allen. I'm grateful to you. Come by the office tomorrow." And without saying good-bye, the pastor hung up.

The next day Reverend March wrote out a check, voicing not a quibble or qualm. Allen transferred the money to Richard Hughes and began waiting out the investment's horizon time.

Business inexplicably improved. A financial analyst of a literary turn of mind claimed that a *carpe diem* mentality accounted for the public's sudden spendthrift ways. Faced with failing energy resources, economic decay, political corruption, the apocalyptic flavor of the times, the public had decided to indulge itself in these last kilowatt days.

The deacon's fund loan and Allen's new customers did not, however, lift Allen's spirits. During this time he sat glumly behind the cash register in his store, his shoulders slumped, the sweep of his hair mussed so that wispy strands hung limply on his high forehead.

Whenever he was alone, especially in the late afternoon, when the accounts had been brought up-to-date, the service calls reported to the independent repairman who took care of his customers, and the store filled with drowsy shadows, Allen fingered the Greek worry beads his wife had given him and thought. The beads were cream colored and speckled, petrified puffed wheat. Rubbing them together between his palms—which assumed the iconographic attitude of prayer—he tried to understand the mystery of his stealing. He felt lost and bounded by this mystery; he was as a blind man thrown into a prison cell. His thoughts dependent upon the texture of events, he searched out the dimensions of his confinement. He recognized that he was materialistic, a sort of acquisitive addict; but labeling his spiritual confusion did not account for it.

By this time Allen had discovered that he did not miss his luxury car or his expensive house, as he had thought he would. No feeling of spiritual liberation accompanied his new living situation, either, but he thought that he might train himself to care for even less, to be content with the necessities of life. He started small. He denied himself the chocolate-covered raisins, beer nuts, and marshmallow-filled cookies he liked to eat while watching TV in the evenings. Still no spiritual elation, but he lost ten pounds.

He had always been a natty dresser, his clothes made of the finest cuts of cloth, his shoes often calfskin. He believed that a short man could make himself more impressive, imposing, by perfecting himself as a physical image. Now he rummaged through his drawers and wore the long-discarded white shirts and chino slacks that he found there to work. He stopped complaining about Stasia's peasant dishes and forced himself to eat blood sausages and chew gristle-filled stew meat. But somehow these measures lacked the bitterness of true renunciation, and so were not curative.

Business continued to be good, and Stasia, who had begun to drop by the store to check on business, wanted to move back into a house—not a grandiose edifice like the last, but a reasonably comfortable place they might rent, where the ceilings did not sparkle.

Allen called Richard Hughes and was assured that soon they would make an "ungodly profit." Allen calculated that he would be able to pay back the church, substantially reduce the principal on his two outstanding loans, and still have enough money for a down payment on a house. Allen met with a real-estate agent and decided upon the price range of houses that Stasia might look at. The new project invigorated Allen and renewed his interest in his business, so that he became the affable salesman again, albeit not a skillful one.

Allen did not tell Stasia about his plans immediately. If she asked about the financing for the house, he had his story prepared: He would tell her that the state legislature had passed a bill which would bring water to his desert property and that he had sold out for a considerable profit. He thought she would accept this; still, she had become so wary that he must find the right time to tell her about the new house.

One night the kids were away, spending the night with friends. Stasia splurgedand served sirloin steak, and they had a romantic dinner. Afterward they sat on the couch in the living room of the apartment, a small room made even cosier, almost claustrophobic in fact, by the presence of the furniture from their old home. Allen decided to tell her.

Stasia exploded. "Even if we can make this down payment," she said, "how do you know that business is going to keep going like it has? The monthly payments are just as bad as they were last time."

"Honey," Allen said, "the economy was in a recession. It's over now."

"Allen, you always do this. You get us into the position of living at the very limit of our means. I don't like it."

"I don't like seeing my wife and girls living in a place like this."

"Why can't the house be a little more modest?"

"I want the best for you, Stasia. Don't you see that?"

"No, not really, Allen, I don't see that. What I see is someone who likes to take risks. Sometimes I think you're some type of gambler. *You're a time-payment craps player!*"

Stasia was so right that Allen wanted to strike her. Instead he left the apartment theatrically, took a stroll, was frightened by an unleashed, snarling Doberman pinscher, and came back and meekly apologized.

Stasia's words, unexpected, raw, accurate, related seemingly disparate actions, revealing the pattern. In

the last two weeks before the investment matured, Allen
returned nightly to his closet, not to pray in the sense of
petitioning the Almighty, but to contemplate the hellishly closed logic of this pattern.

If his acquisitive addiction stemmed from a desire to
gamble, then the only way of renunciation that would
suffice would be to give up the control of his affairs. But
he was an independent businessman; Stasia and his
daughters rightly expected him to provide for them as
well as he was able. He would have to continue with his
business, suffering daily temptation, like an alcoholic
forced to take one drink each day and then expected to
remain sober. Yet there in the closet, afraid that Stasia
would discover him, afraid that God had long ago abandoned him to his own desires, he still hoped that repay-
ment of the church would dispel this vision of the future
as a daily crucifixion, that he would be forgiven, allowed
to live in his old, self-forgetful way.

The futures investment matured. As Richard Hughes
predicted, Allen made an ungodly profit of thirty-five
thousand dollars.

So Allen found himself one Sunday morning—a year
and three months after embarking on his criminal
odyssey—standing at the back of the sanctuary, waiting
fretfully for Reverend March to end his sermon, so that
he might repay the church in the privacy of the business
office. The sum he had made on the deacon's fund investment, which exceeded even his Sybaritic imagin-
ings, troubled him. If he were God, he would not have
allowed Allen Gresham to have so manifestly profited

from speculating—gambling—with funds meant for the poor.

At last Reverend March concluded his sermon with one of his favorite rhetorical devices, a question twice repeated. He asked: "Are you ready to lay your all on the altar? Well, are you?" And then he prayed. Allen knew that as the altar call started, during the first verse of the invitation hymn, the counsellors for the newly converted, even if there were no converts, would make their way down the aisles to the door which led into small offices where the counsellors might meet with those who came forward. There would be movement, and Allen might duck out and head toward the business office. The pastor said amen, the congregation began to sing "Beneath the Cross of Jesus," and Allen exited.

Allen performed his accounting tasks—except for entering the final total—and then he took his checkbook from the breast pocket of his corduroy sports jacket. He did not write out his check, but waited for a signal—a sign—the merest tip of God's metaphysical cap. He looked at the wall before him. The poster still hung there, the finger-painted sun and the inscription "God Loves You." Allen needed to feel that love; now, immediately.

He felt nothing except an aggravating fear. He must leave soon; if the moment passed uneventfully, he would go away doomed, his life predictable and yet unforeseen, a Greek tragedy. Like an actor opening the channel of an emotion within himself, Allen tried to evoke the feeling of God's love by remembering the time he had felt that love. (As a salesman, he was more adept at this than might be supposed.) He remembered

that moment when he felt that Jesus, in beckoning Zacchaeus to come down from the tree, had turned His sight
upon Allen, recognized him, made him understand that
he was known and loved. He tried to cry again as he had
that day. His eyes did start to water, his sinuses inflated.
He reached for the checkbook and remembered the end
of the story. Zacchaeus had repaid his victims four times
over. Allen had stolen about seven thousand dollars from
the offering and deacon's fund, he had made twenty-
eight thousand.

He was stunned; it was very much as if he had been
deftly punched. Then slowly, waiting for the passage of
time to reassure him that he was himself and that the
world had reassumed its usual, unobtrusive, passive
character, he began to think. The circumstance of the
one-hundred-dollar bill had led him into stealing. He
had wrongly interpreted this circumstance as revealing
God's will. How could he be sure that the magic of this
fourfold multiplication revealed God's will?

He wanted to negotiate. He recollected his prayers
and how they had led him to see the entrapment of his
acquisitive addiction. Would giving the church all the
money really liberate him from his time-payment gambling, lifting him out of that hellishly circular logic? He
wished another sign, omen, portent had accompanied
this revelation. If he remembered the end of Zacchaeus'
story now, he had remembered the story about the coin
in the fish's mouth that first Sunday. God seemed aw-
fully greedy: He wanted everything. How would Allen
come up with the money to pay the capital-gains tax? It
would be an incredible risk.

Allen wrote out a check for seven thousand dollars,

deposited it and the rest of the day's offering in the floor safe, and left the office. Soon thereafter, he initiated a plan by which he sought to avoid temptation. He gave over the control of their financial affairs to Stasia. And he resigned from his position as head usher and took his seat in the congregation with his family.

Christbirth

WARREN COATES AWOKE one Sunday morning in early December and began to prepare himself to teach his Sunday-school class for ten-year-old boys at the First Baptist Church of San Cariño in Los Angeles. Still in his pajamas, he went into the bathroom. He stood before the medicine-cabinet mirror, washed his face, and then shaved, his double-bladed razor making long, even strokes. With the arch of his high forehead set above the ground of his firm jaw, his brown hair, and deeply set hazel eyes, Warren was an attractive man in his early sixties and the perfect image of a paterfamilias.

He went back into his bedroom and put on his gray suit. The suit was new and made of that comfortable double-knit material, but he did not like it very much. They cut clothes these days for skinny fellows with no behinds at all. His wife, Helen, always had said that he had a "monumental" figure, like a sculpted horseman from the Renaissance. By comparing him to a work of art, she had made him feel so alive. But Helen had been dead now for over two years.

He went to the hall closet, opened the double doors,

39

and pulled out a cloth-lined drawer designed to hold silverware. But in this drawer lay a large, purple velvet bag that opened and closed with a tasselled drawstring. Warren had sewn this bag together during his spare hours at the fire-station house. In this bag were to be found, as in the other three drawers in similar bags, the line drawings of Helen Coates.

The Coates's considerable success over the years with the children in their Sunday-school classes was in part due to these drawings, each of which illustrated a story from the Scriptures upon which the lesson for a given Sunday might be based. There had been a drawing for every Sunday in the year, but two or three had been misplaced or stolen during Helen's lifetime, and now that she was gone, Warren had become reluctant to use them.

Warren had been having trouble, however, holding his class's attention, so he thought he should use the drawings again. This week's lesson was about Jesus as a twelve-year-old boy talking with the teachers of the synagogue at Jerusalem, and Warren thought Helen's drawing of this scene one of her finest.

Warren transferred the drawing to the wooden attaché-sized case in which Helen had stored her paints and which he had cleaned and refinished and made into a travelling ark for the drawings. He looked at his watch and, seeing that he had a few extra minutes, he decided to take his Bible and Sunday-school lesson book into the living room and sit for a while.

Helen had persuaded him that, since their two daughters were grown and married, they ought to move to this apartment, where they might more comfortably live on his fireman's pension and her art-teacher's salary, and which they might furnish for themselves, instead of for the children. And so they had moved and Helen had created this living room, this sanctuary. Its oriental rugs covered shining hardwood floors. Swedish chairs, their backs made of wood with a grain of infinite fineness, and two short couches covered with chrysanthemum yellow brocade formed a decorous semicircle before the fireplace. Above the mantel hung the Dürer etching Helen had found on their trip to Europe and later verified as an original. His wife's oversized art books—plate-filled volumes on Rembrandt, Ingres, Daumier, Goya, and others—stood on the wall shelves Warren had put up.

Warren believed that Helen's presence would never depart from this place. And that is why—though his daughters thought it morbid—he had placed "candid" framed photographs of Helen all about the room. These photographs stood among the books, on the four end tables next to the couches, on the sideboard in the adjoining dining room, and on the crescent table just off the entryway. His favorite photograph of Helen he reserved for the mantel; he placed it next to the rose-colored Venetian glass vase he had taken out of storage and which he constantly replenished with flowers.

It was time to go. He grabbed up his Bible and lesson book off the coffee table and took his ritual parting look at the photograph of Helen on the entryway table. The photograph had been taken at their eldest daughter's wedding and caught the mother of the bride regarding her daughter; Helen's smile, its wistfulness, revealed a longing to reenact the long drama of marriage. Her smile assured Warren that, despite time and circumstance, she would go with him.

Outside the apartment, he saw that poinsettias had bloomed among the bird of paradise along the walk. Fitzgerald, who owned the building across the street, had already put up Christmas lights.

By the time the boys began to arrive, Warren had set the drawing on the easellike chalkboard stand in the Sunday-school room. He had placed his Bible and lesson book on the frail lectern, arranged the twelve metal folding chairs in three rows, which comfortably filled the room, and opened the window a bit.

As they came in, the more conscientious boys recited the Bible verse he had asked them to memorize for that Sunday. They were all soon assembled, squirming in their seats, Warren thought, like worms trying to dig into a hiding place. They shot looks up at Warren and at the drawing; all except Greg Jackson, who sat in an uncharacteristic, dejected silence, his hands balled up in the pockets of his blue and green plaid cardigan, his snap-on tie askew.

Warren's present difficulty with holding the class's attention was chiefly due to Greg Jackson's antics. Greg had disrupted Warren's class for so many weeks that the other boys came to class waiting to see some type of duel between teacher and pupil. These duels took several forms: Greg started a fight with another boy or made flatulent noises; one time he set a church bulletin on fire, but most often he simply argued with Warren. Greg's short curly brown hair—which made the top of his head look exceptionally flat—and his pointed chin made Warren think of the expression "sharp as a tack." But he doubted it was really intelligence which caused Greg to make such a nuisance of himself. Greg's case particularly troubled Warren, for in the past he had always had a way with boisterous kids. In fact, since his wife and he had only two daughters, he had come to think of his favorite boys from over the years—many of whom had at first acted like Greg—as adopted sons. Many of his favorites had grown up and moved to other parts of the country, but they still sent him cards on his birthday.

Warren began speaking, and in a very short while, he knew that the magic of the drawing was working. The boys sat still and listened.

When Helen had first suggested they might use her art in their classes, even Warren thought that she had become too involved with her own way of looking at things. But the night she had shown him the first drawing, a drawing of the story of Baalam's ass, he had found himself transfixed by Helen's exposition of how the picture told the story. The drawing consisted almost entirely of outline, the only details provided being the ones which carried the weight of the story. In the case of Baalam's ass, Helen had completed the faces of the donkey and Baalam, revealing the essential transfigurations of the beast into a perceiver of the divine and of the man into an animal blinded by stubbornness and anger to the angel before him. The angel had not been drawn, because one had to identify with Baalam in order to truly understand the story.

Though Helen had explained that what she had done depended upon the long iconographic tradition, especially as it had been transformed by the naturalistic

Flemish, Warren believed his wife to be the most crea-
tive creature in existence. And soon after, when he saw
that his boys were as interested in the drawings as he, a
certain awe entered his love for his wife.

That Sunday the boys' interest increased as Warren
described how the postures and gestures of the various
teachers grouped about Jesus depicted their reactions to
the child's great wisdom. The teachers came alive for the
boys as they identified with them.

Soon, the boys politely interrupted Warren to offer that
that man to the left, gesturing outside the circle, was
calling others to witness the spectacle, and the one with
a smug grin had just posed a question he thought too
difficult for Jesus to answer. And the two figures in the
background were Mary and Joseph, who had left Jesus
behind and to whom—when His parents asked Him why
He had stayed behind—Jesus replied that He had to be
about His Father's business. Then Warren explained
that the man with his hand to his mouth was contemplating the great mystery Jesus presented. This wise man
knew Jesus was doing God's work. And if Jesus as a boy
did God's work, the boys of Mr. Coates's class ought to
be doing the same.

Class time was about over; all the classes of children
from nine to eleven years of age would gather in an assembly for the last half of the Sunday-school hour. If
Warren allowed questions, Greg might yet make trouble.
But the lesson had gone well; Warren thought he might
risk it. Greg raised his hand, as expected, but so did two
others. Warren answered their questions first. But finally, with almost no time remaining, Greg spoke.

"But wasn't that a sin? I mean, wasn't it bad for Jesus

to get lost like that? How much should we obey our parents?"

"I'm afraid," Warren said, "that's a kettle of fish we really don't have time to get into. It's a matter of allegiance; you obey a captain before you obey a lieutenant. Maybe we'll talk about it next week. Right now we'd better go into assembly."

"But I want you to answer." Greg was on his feet. He appeared slightly comic, as children do when they are entirely serious. In Greg's almond-eyed stare there was a brooding desperation that Warren had never seen before. Still, it was late, and Warren had finally conducted an orderly class, and he was somewhat desperate himself that Greg should not cause a fracas now.

"I have to dismiss class now, Greg. Please sit down, We'll have prayer, and then we *will* go into assembly."

Warren closed his eyes and bowed his head and waited for the room to quiet. But heard Greg's shoes click on the linoleum.

"I want you to answer!" Greg screamed, his voice singing in the shrill upper registers. "You never listen to me. You hate me."

Warren finally opened his eyes. He looked down on Greg's olive-skinned face. Greg's eyebrows were not pinched, his mouth was not twisted or set in any way; rather, the boy's face was uncannily calm, stonelike. And as Warren, with a strange feeling of wonder, gazed at Greg, the boy's face seemed to take on meaning in much the same way the faces in the line drawings did. The boy's face at once resisted and demanded explanation. Warren felt as if his mind, like blind hands, held the image of the face to know it. And then, suddenly, he saw

with Greg's eyes and knew that Greg was absolutely
right. He hated Greg. And he hated him with no simple
hatred, but one which sounded his deepest motivations.
He became conscious of his own body, of his bulky presence, as a threat.

"Please, Greg," he said, "please sit down."

But Greg moved toward the easel. Warren was somehow certain that the boy intended to destroy the drawing, and so Warren struck him; struck him with his open
hand, knocking him against the wall. Greg did not cry.
He kept silent and crouched against the wall. Warren
asked the other boys to take their chairs and leave the
room. "Quickly," he said, "please."

Warren shut the door against the hubbub in the assembly room and sat Greg in a chair. He asked the boy to
forgive him. He said that the drawing had been done by
his wife, who was now dead, and that he feared Greg was
going to harm it. (Explaining this, he realized how unreasonable, even disturbed, his premonition revealed
him to be.) Warren explained that he did not hate
Greg—he knew he was lying, but it would certainly not
have been more kind to tell the truth—but that his questions did try Warren's patience. Greg must try not to ask
so many questions, especially the ones he asked just for
the sake of argument.

"You hate me," Greg said. "You hate me. You never
listen to me." The boy began to cry.

Warren was so distraught that he could not think of
anything to say. He left the room and found Phillip
Henderson, another teacher, and asked him to see Greg
home. Warren could not explain, but Greg must be
helped. Warren excused himself and left.

Warren arrived home and sat in his living room, trying to calm down and think this thing out. But there, where he had always felt a tremendous freedom, as if he were a performer utterly sure of his part, he felt oppressed. He saw that the harmony of Helen's decor had been destroyed by his Venetian glass vase and the photographs of Helen. Instead of seeing how the photographs caught Helen's characteristic expressions, he became conscious of the deficiencies of these images: the way her eyes looked red in one, the exaggeration of the bump at the bridge of her nose in another. He still did not see them as morbid, as did his daughters, but they now ached with their lifelessness.

The lifelessness of the photographs caused him to suffer. He seemed to be suddenly conscious of the very life in his flesh. And this life was at once itself and an agony. Then the pain seemed to leave him, but as it did, he recognized it for the presence of Helen. At that moment he quite expected to die. But, of course, he did not.

He became angry then; his face darkened, became a mask of brutal resignation. The still presence of his home, which was no longer his home but an arrangement of empty space and objects, testified to what had been with all the terrible incompleteness of a lone, perfect Aeolian column. Seeing the ruins, Warren thought to destroy it completely. *But ashes cannot be burned,* he thought. There were the drawings.

He found old newspaper in the kitchen, brought out two sawdust composition logs from the storage bin hidden in the living room wall beside the bookcase, opened the flue, and made a small fire. He took the three purple velvet sacks out of their drawers and, coming back into the living room, set them on the coffee table before the couch. He began burning the drawings. They darkened as they felt the heat, seeming to liquefy at their centers. Their edges arched upward, turning into scalloped, fire-tipped circles; before they disintegrated, they might have been the flowers of Sheol. There were many drawings, and it took a long time for them all to be burned.

Warren sat back down on the couch. The room seemed to recede from him. He felt as if he were sitting in a train, waiting to pull out of the station on the first leg of a long journey. He must say good-bye, but he had only one person who might hear him or be interested. And so he said, *All right, God. I forgive You.*

The time began to pass. Warren remained seated on the couch, not asleep or awake but in a kind of spiritual catatonia.

In the early evening, Warren roused himself. Trying to put his thoughts in order, he remembered his prayer. To hate God as he had: beyond what he could feel, know, or imagine, he sensed to be the cardinal order of his sin. And yet he felt nothing more than embarrassment, as if he were a boy caught in a boastful lie. If he asked, he believed he would be forgiven, but he thought he should wait until this sheepish feeling had been replaced by remorse.

He must begin again, though. He did not know if he could ever truly love Greg or recapture the paternal feeling he once had for his Sunday-school boys. But there were his daughters and grandchildren. He had not seen them much since their mother's death, especially here at the apartment. They thought he had made the place into a mausoleum, and in order not to hear that, he had stopped inviting them. He might make amends, he thought, by having them all over for Christmas. He would clean and cook and do all the things his girls ran themselves off their feet doing.

And so, though his party would not take place for another three and one-half weeks, Warren began to make preparations. He took down most of Helen's photographs and set up photographs of his daughters and their families on the living room end tables. Then he searched the storage closet and found the boxes which contained the Christmas decorations. He took the box which housed the crèche into the living room. There he began to unwrap the painted, plaster-of-paris shepherds and wise men. He removed the balsa-wood manger and discovered underneath it a sheet of heavy vellum: Helen's drawing of the Nativity. He felt the strength go from his legs and arms. He sat down and wept.

The Missionary Conference

I WALK INTO THE LIVING ROOM and turn on the standing lamp beside the couch. It sheds a harsh, inexhaustible light, the light of all lamps at this hour, 4:00 A.M. My eyes smart, a headache begins; I want nothing more than to return to bed. My wife and young son are asleep, our apartment is small, so I am careful not to make too much noise. I think of taking a book from the shelves, but I know I cannot concentrate at these times.

I have just had a dream, a recurring nightmare. I cannot remember the dream itself, and yet I know what it was about, or at least its origin, and thus something of its meaning. I'll explain.

While I was growing up, Dr. Peter Lynn came once every four years to hold a missionary conference in our suburban church, the First Baptist Church of San Cariño. He conducted these conferences to raise money for his ministry in the Belgian Congo.

I was eleven years old when the Lynns came for the second time. Before, Mrs. Lynn had accompanied her husband, but this time only Dr. Lynn and his son Randy were coming. The Lynns stayed in our home because Dr. Lynn and my mother grew up together and attended the same church in Chicago. Also, as I learned later, my mother insisted on their staying with us because she was quite an intelligent woman, and she enjoyed talking with a man who did not share my father's reactionary sensibilities.

And so, on Friday afternoon my parents and I drove down the San Diego Freeway toward the Los Angeles International Airport at seventy-five miles per hour in my father's white Chevy Impala. The interior smelled of dust because my father worked as a building contractor. He drove with one hand atop the two-tone, white and burgundy steering wheel. The other hand, resting on his leg, was saved for turns and emergencies. I could see his blond flat top, gleaming with the butch wax like a bed of needles. My mother sat at the opposite end of the front bench seat. Her dark, lustrous hair was cut short. From my position in the backseat, I could see her delicately fluted nose and one of her agate-hard, hazel eyes when she turned in profile to speak with my father.

We arrived at the airport, parked the car, and soon were looking at one of the great boards that posted information about the latest arrivals or departures. I heard the *chich, chich, chich* of the mechanical letters changing on the board. We checked the fact that the plane from Chicago was on time against one of the airport's clocks. We had arrived a good half hour before the plane was due, but we proceeded immediately down the long, wide corridor toward the gate area.

I remember that corridor. Silver lines separated the

white floor into rectangular blocks of ersatz marble, white tiles covered the walls, and the voice of the woman who announced arrivals and departures seemed no voice at all, but simply the sound of the corridor. It was an enchanted place—magic—it made me feel as if I were passing out of my world and might emerge into another. I knew that at the end of the corridor lay the airplanes, great cylindrical containers of possibility.

We sat in the swivel bucket chairs at the gate and waited. I stared out the windows at the yellow markings where the plane would stop and thought about Randy. I had never met anyone with whom I had become friends so effortlessly as I had with Randy. We had spent three weeks together that summer four years ago, and though he had been a year older, he had been a perfect peer. He was coordinated and athletic, but no more so than I was, so that we truly could not tell who would be able to run faster or hit a baseball farther. I was counting on him to help me in my street-football rivalry with Myron Brodsky—my consuming interest at the time.

The plane taxied into position. We waited with the small crowd that had gathered, tried to see Dr. Lynn and Randy step off the plane onto the mobile, now-positioned stairway, looked to the door in case they had escaped notice. Then they were with us, Dr. Lynn and Randy.

Now Randy looked like his older brother, Timothy, as I remembered him. Nearly as tall as his father, taller than mine, he was spider thin. He used Vitalis on his thick, russet hair. His cheeks looked dirty, somehow shadowed. Then I saw that the shadows were composed of whorling down that had yet to stiffen into whiskers. He had acne, too.

He patted me on the shoulder and put his arm around me. I did not know how to respond. Then it hit me: I would be Johnny Unitas launching the football as Randy, like Raymond Berry, made his cut toward the corner of the end zone, and the ball would find those long-fingered hands like a bird alighting.

I greeted him fervently.

That night, after dinner, we lingered at the table while the adults drank their coffee. It both amazed and bored me, with backaching boredom, how adults could linger at a dinner table talking their talk. And so I was relieved when Mom said we could go watch TV, if we liked. But then Randy asked if he might have a cup of coffee, and I thought he had foiled our escape and was embarrassed that he should ask such a thing. But Mother smiled, and in the quiet way she had of bringing off surprises, said matter-of-factly that she would bring two cups into the den. She brought the tray, and after pouring Randy's cup and adding milk, she asked didn't I like it with both milk and sugar and then she doctored it as best she could. Still, the coffee tasted the way coffee tastes the first time you have it, which, as I remember it, is something like essence of tree bark.

But I sipped at it, dangling my pinkie and wondering who Randy thought he was. He soon told me. He told me of his life at the boarding school for missionaries' kids in Stanleyville. He thought it made one mature faster to live away from one's home and family. Then he spoke

French for me, and I acted impressed. (I did like the sound of the feminine vowels and the uvular r's.) He told me of his dislike for most things American, including hamburgers, and how he deplored the wasteful ways of Americans, who buy plastic boxes in which to hide Kleenex tissue boxes at a price which would buy a day's food for an entire family in Congo. I asked him if he wouldn't like to watch TV—Red Skelton was about to come on. He *never* watched TV. "Besides, Buddy," he said (he called me *buddy*, a real gaffe in my social circle), "let's talk." And he smiled his long, ambling line of a smile.

There was a lull. Randy tweezed a pimple between thumb and forefinger, I popped my knuckles and tried to think of a topic of conversation. I had lately begun to read the paper and occasionally listened to my parents talk about politics. I remembered my mom saying something about the communists and the Simbas in the Congo, so I recited my dad's John Bircher argument for maintaining the global line of defense against the communists. Randy said that it was different when you lived with the communists. He agreed that they were evil atheists, but he said you can see some of their points when you see what capitalism had done in a country like Congo. "We must understand each other's point of view," he said.

Then Randy looked at me, fixing my eyes with a deep, soul-searching gaze. He told me that he thought our generation would make the decisions that would lead to world peace or nuclear war and the final extinction of mankind.

"Yes," I said, and closed my eyes to escape his hypnotic stare. Thoughts about the Rapture and the Second Coming and the Millennium and how what Randy said did not square with Baptist eschatology troubled me for a moment. Then I said, "Even I have important decisions to make. I have to decide which socks to put on in the morning, and between tuna and sandwich spread for lunch." He was on me then, and we wrestled and laughed on the floor long enough to find out that he was *much* stronger, but that I was quicker, too quick to be pinned.

"Come on," I said, crouched on my knees and out of his reach. "Let's watch Red Skelton."

Randy and I did not have to attend all the Saturday missionary-conference sessions at the church. Mom suggested that we spend the morning at the house and after lunch, which we would find in the refrigerator, we should peddle over on the two bikes to see the slide presentation. (I remember my red rocket bicycle had baseball cards attached to the wheels so that the spokes made a ripping, enginelike noise.)

We arrived on time at one-thirty, found the conference room in the graying lath-and-plaster, two-story Sunday-school building, and entered to see about sixty people seated in folding chairs in front of a portable movie screen. The room smelled of the soapy punch the church always served at functions.

The slide presentation began with the obligatory shot out the airplane window, showing jet engines attached to a wing above a bed of clouds. There were slides of the airport at Leopoldville and slides of the city itself, the hues dominated by the green and red washes of color slides in the early sixties. Very white doctors and missionaries in safari shorts were shown standing together before the small, square hospital among a ring of Africans. In the next slide, these same people collectively pointed at the steeple of the new church, which lay in an ugly clearing. We saw the girls in the sewing class, their black faces happy and bewildered and truly looking into the camera, rather than posing.

The slides came to an end and Dr. Lynn began to talk. He stood behind a table on which he had arranged a display of witch-doctor rattles, a ceremonial costume, a stuffed elephant's foot, a machetelike weapon, and a python skin.

Dr. Lynn said that the python skin came from a snake that had been killed after he attempted to eat one of the boys from a neighboring village. The snake had tripped the boy up, swallowed his feet, and was gradually pulling more and more of the boy into his gullet. The boy screamed for help, but no one heard. As he was about to be totally consumed, it occurred to the boy that if he held his arms straight out from his shoulders, the snake would not be able to open his mouth wide enough to swallow him. This worked. Dr. Lynn made theological hay out of this story in two ways: He compared the boy to Jonah, and he talked about the sign of the cross and redemption.

He also told a tale about an insect called a *mombt*, whose bite was absolutely fatal and was particularly sinister in that the poison injected by the insect lay dormant for one year and only then, but very suddenly, caused death.

Dr. Lynn concluded by advising us that we should not think of missionaries as romantic pioneers in a Tarzan movie; we should think of them as workers for Christ, assisting an indigenous people (we were never to say *natives* again) to establish a church.

At the last, Dr. Lynn had minimized the exotic incidents in his work. But as I listened to his talk, I imagined pirogues, weaver birds, and sobi grass, and I heard the strange rhythms of heavily consonated Kikongo, the Bantu language of the people with whom he worked and the language in which he recited the Lord's Prayer. It was the very foreignness of these things which made them loci of the imagination—vacuums asking to be filled. As I went off to play street football, this other world beckoned, and yet I was happy to return to my own.

By the time we had all the players assembled on my front lawn, it was midafternoon. The sun appeared intermittently through the clouds on that late fall day.

Myron and I chose up teams.

I picked Randy, out of courtesy rather than because of any Johnny U. and Raymond Berry dream. When we had begun knocking on doors, rounding up players, Randy had made a show of the soccer stunts he could perform, insisting that he did not know why we were to play *fooseball* with such an odd-shaped thing. He kicked it a tremendous distance and then kept it in the air and close before him by kicking it with first his right, then his left, foot. He threw the ball, however, like a girl—from the elbow instead of the shoulder. And he dropped many of the little flips I tossed him as we made our way down the street.

Myron, standing almost as tall as Randy, his brown hair combed to the side, where it flowered into a mass of tight curls, spun the ball in his hands, looked over the draftees with the air of a poker player who has just been dealt his fourth ace, and picked Vincent. Vincent was a moderately tall, moderately fat Italian guy who, though not overly fast, could both throw and catch.

I picked Jim, who was as tall as my father and weighed more. He was the cliché fat kid with the wonderful heart incarnate. No one was happier than I (except perhaps Jim himself) when he continued growing, slimmed down, and became the best fullback in the history of our local high school.

Myron picked Phillip, who looked like a great athlete—broad shoulders, long legs—but who played lackadaisically. Phillip lived in a trance; it was as if he had been born but had never quite come to life.

I picked Sheldon next—a tall, thin fellow who wore pocketless sailor denims. Sheldon's head looked under-inflated. We had given him the nickname Rutabaga. He was a reliable end on short patterns.

Donald—splayfooted Donald—fell to Myron and so trudged off with our opponents to receive the kickoff. Everyone felt sorry for Donald because he was such a clod and was always picked last, but everyone hated him, too. Donald knew everyone felt sorry for him, and so, when he did by chance hook up with the winning team, he gloated; at the age of thirteen, he had mastered the art of being obnoxious.

The length and width of the street between three tele-

phone poles constituted the playing field. The rules
were: Two-hand touch below the neck downed the run-
ner, all players were eligible to catch a pass, advancing
beyond the middle telephone pole was a first down, as
was the reception of two passes within any one series of
downs. Wide open, blissful street football.

The game soon became another battle between Myron
and me.

Ever since I had moved to the neighborhood about
three years before, Myron and I had been close friends,
but it was a friendship born of dissimilarity and nurtured
by rivalry. Myron had Reformed Jewish parents, but he
was the most *Jewish* Jewish person I knew. His father
spoke Yiddish. We often discussed religion, and not in
an ecumenical spirit. Each thought the other's beliefs
wrongheaded, crazy, stupid—that's what made the ar-
guments so enjoyable.

Myron was a year older than I, and, always somewhat
taller, he had recently beanstalked a good six inches.
About the time he did so, the personal battles started.
The teams seemed to keep matching up evenly, if Myron
and I were considered of equal ability—as we always
had been—and Myron, with his new height and speed
advantage, had led his team to victory every time. Myron
knew that by winning these games he laid claim to an
absolute superiority over me. To me, it was as if he had
an unbreakable hold on one of the "pressure points" the
judo experts talked about then. During these games we
thought of ourselves as the truest of ancient foes. Street
football became a struggle of will against will, being
against being; an icon, I suppose, of our Nietzschean
camaraderie. I laugh now that I remember it so clearly,

and yet, it had its own integrity.

That day Myron made several miscalculations. When he saw Randy drop the first several passes, he thought he had the game won. But Jim had begun to acquire the coordination that would later make him an all-city fullback. When it became certain that Randy could not catch and could not remember the difference between a Z-out and a banana-left pass pattern, I substituted Jim for myself at quarterback, switched Randy to center, and made myself an end. Except that, when we ran the ball, I took the snap and had Jim block for me. This offense worked because, as Myron had outgrown me, he had become overly confident in his pure speed and did not see that he had lost the quickness that my compact little frame retained. I kept beating him on button-hook-and-go patterns. And Jim could fairly launch the old pigskin, so Myron had to stay with me, and this opened up short passes to Sheldon.

When the streetlights went on, the two teams were tied, and our team had the ball. By the rules, when the streetlights went on, the team that had the ball was allowed to run out its downs, and then the game was over. (We settled on this rule because the members of the leading team would often go quickly home when their mothers called them, proclaiming victory, and there would ensue a lot of screaming about quitters and finks.) So we had one more chance to score, and the ball was just beyond the middle telephone pole.

I ran with the ball, Jim knocked Phillip and Donald down, Sheldon fenced out Vincent, I grabbed hold of Randy's belt, and, pushing him into Myron, slithered through the gap and ran for the end zone. Myron caught me from behind, as I knew he would, but it was a terrific gain.

On second down, I ran a post pattern and Jim threw the ball toward me at the sideline in the end zone. I knew that the Cheverton's ground-cover ivy carpeted the out-of-bounds sideline, so I tried to skim my feet over the earth in Raymond Berry fashion and make a falling catch. This was one of my better moves, and when I saw others do it, I thought it a beautiful thing to behold. There was one problem; if you jumped too far into the ivy and landed face down, you were liable to get a mouthful of sprinkler. I caught the ball and fell into the ivy. I came up with my teeth in place, but my feet had left the ground, and even I had to admit that I was out-of-bounds when I made the catch. On third down I ran the ball again and made it to within five yards of the goal line.

Back in the huddle I considered whether to try another run or a pass. I could see Myron pacing in the end zone, trying to look bored, one hand on his hip; I knew he was dying, and I was filled with joy. This would be the first victory over him, if I could only call the right play. Finally, I said, "Okay, this is it, gang," or some such Johnny U. words, and explained the last play slowly.

Randy hiked the ball to me, and I started to run to the left behind Sheldon. But before I crossed the line of scrimmage, I lateraled the ball back to Jim, who had retreated from his end position into quarterback territory. Then Sheldon and I took off toward the right-hand corner of the end zone. I knew that Myron would think we were trying to flood his zone with two receivers, providing a screen and springing one of us into the clear. I also counted on him believing that I would not trust Sheldon to catch a pass in such a critical situation. As expected, Myron abandoned Sheldon, screaming at Vincent to cover him and at Phillip and Donald to rush the passer. Somehow I broke into the clear two steps ahead of the screaming Myron and yelled for the ball. Jim cocked his arm, I leaped, skimmed over the earth, and fell into the ivy. Myron fell on top of me.

I yelled for Myron to get off. He looked at me and, seeing that I did not have the ball, rolled off me and looked for the ball in the ivy. Then he looked at Sheldon, who didn't have the ball, either. He saw me looking to the opposite sideline. There, holding the ball in one hand over his head, grinning absurdly, stood Randy. He was incredibly pleased with himself for having scored. Except, as I saw and tried not to let on to, he had *not* scored. He had not actually crossed the goal line, but stood two feet within the playing field. Myron yelled. Seeing Donald coming at him, Randy finally took the last stride and was instantly tagged.

"Touchdown!" I screamed. Myron ran over to Donald and asked him in an authoritarian voice whether or not he had tagged Randy before he crossed the goal line. Donald said he did.

Myron waved his hands back and forth across one another—for some reason making the sign of an incomplete pass—and announced, "Sorrrr-ry, no touch-down."

I ran over to him, screaming "Bullpucky!" I asked Randy if he had scored. He said he could not be sure. (Ah, betrayed by that diplomat!) I turned to Jim, who loudly pronounced touchdown, as did Sheldon.

Myron said, "Your own man isn't sure. No-o-o-o touchdown." I turned back to Randy. His grin had turned into tight-lipped silence. Myron started walking toward his house.

I went crazy. I ran after him, screaming "We won! Admit it! Admit it!"

He kept replying airily, "Your own man, Son. I'm sorry."

I positioned myself in front of him, stood my ground in good Western (*circa* Rod Taylor) style, and said firmly, "You're going to admit we won."

"No way," he said. "No way." And he gave me a shove.

"You *are*, you geek!"

"Listen whimp . . . ." And he shoved me again.

A moment of serene, silent violence seemed to clear my mind of all thoughts. I threw my fist into his face: I did not clip his jaw—I put my fist squarely into his cheekbone and followed through toward the back of his skull. He actually fell over. It took me one unreal moment, but then I realized what I had done, a thing heretofore unseen and implicitly taboo—the neighborhood kids shoved, wrestled, occasionally socked each other in the arm or the stomach—but we never threw haymakers to the face. I started running.

Myron caught me and threw me into the Cheverton's ivy, where he began to choke me. His knees were right at my shoulder sockets, which caused considerable pain and rendered my arms two waving tentacles. He exerted enough pressure on my throat to choke off the air and made my Adam's apple send knifelike pains into my throat. I decided I could wait him out: Jim was sure to rescue me.

But very soon, perhaps because I had been running and was breathless anyway, my vision blurred. Myron hovered indistinctly above me. The pressure on my throat continued and, being my last link with the conscious world, it became somehow reassuring. I was terrified then, so I gave one last jerk of my legs and arms, twisted to the side, so that my face was buried in the ivy roots, and tried (with the effort of any struggle for life) to pull a bit of air into my lungs. I do not know if any air reached my lungs; I know only that I smelled the water and mint smell of the ivy and the humic soil.

Then I passed out.

I regained consciousness—Jim finally decided I had had enough and threw Myron off me—but I did not become lucid until I was being carried up my driveway with Jim on one side, Sheldon on the other, my arms draped over their necks—the ritual method of trucking players off the field. Everyone followed in a horseshoe cluster, including Myron, and we moved like an indecisive crab. When I understood that they intended to deliver me like that to my mother, I insisted on being put down and told everyone to go home, I was fine. They were reluctant. I repeated myself angrily. They knew I was okay then and left.

I remember catching sight of Myron's face before he turned back to his house. He wore an aloof expression, but he lingered a moment for a sign. My hands before my chest, I made a condensed version of the touchdown signal. He smirked, shrugged a "Maybe," and walked off.

When we went into my house, Randy tried to apologize—for exactly what, we were both not sure—but I told him to leave me alone and went off to my room. There my emotions caught up with me; the shaking started in my chest, and I stifled any possible sounds of sobbing by flexing my stomach muscles as if to defend myself against punches to the midsection. Then I could not come out of my room, because I did not want my family and Randy to see I had been crying. In fact, I thought I never wanted to see Randy again. That evening, after I had calmed down, Randy and I watched TV together in a silence that drowned out the laugh tracks.

When it was time to go to the Sunday-evening church service, I was glad that Randy had to sit up front so that he could join his father in shaking hands with the congregation after the service.

I sat in my usual place in a right rear pew. The service was extraordinarily crowded—the church sanctuary held about five hundred people, and all the pews were filled. I was afraid the old Missouri Baptist lady who sat next to me would touch my arm and tell me to face front. But she refrained, and with my pen and the Sunday bulletin propped on a hymnal, I successfully doodled my way through the baptisms, the song service, the love offering for the Lynns' ministry, the announcements, the offering, the special soprano solo, and halfway through the sermon.

Then Dr. Lynn mentioned the *mombt* insect again, and I started listening. In his brown sharkskin suit, standing against the backdrop of the empty choir pews with one hand set on the Spurgeon rail of the pulpit, Dr.

Lynn looked like the dignified former seminary professor he was. He lectured rather than preached, his voice rising and falling, insinuating subtleties.

He talked of the Congo that night, of the crying need for doctors and teachers and Bible translators and preachers to come and minister to those who were hungry for the message of Jesus Christ. He told stories of young boys whose marks on a crucial exam were one or two points below the cutoff line. They had to go back to their villages and abandon any hope of education beyond their grammar-school training. Though they cried on his doorstep for days, there simply were not enough high-school teachers to take all but the top 2 or 3 percent. He told of women with goiters the size of grapefruits, of men with elephantiasis, and of the existence of huge leper colonies.

His voice deepened as it became more inspired. He evoked a vision of the Congo inhabited by those strange lovers: terror and beauty.

Then he followed the one line of reasoning which transformed his message into a plea aimed directly at me. He talked of the arduous and treacherous road one had to take in order to become a missionary. He spoke of years of college, years of medical training, years of seminary work, and then the impossibility of knowing until the last whether or not the mission board would commission you to go and whether or not you would be able to raise, from your local churches, the support funds that you would need to survive in the bush. Good Lord! At that age if there was one thing I could not resist, it was a challenge.

He talked finally of the political unrest in the Congo. He said he did not know whether, after returning to the

Congo this spring, he would ever return to the United States again. But he could say with the Apostle Paul, "For me to live is Christ and to die is gain." He asked us if we could say the same.

After Dr. Lynn prayed, he led the congregation in singing the invitation hymn, "So Send I You." The first verse began:

> So send I you to labor for the Master
> So send I you to work for God alone . . . .

He asked us to hum the next verse while he pleaded with the young people in the congregation to come forward and commit themselves to a life of full-time Christian service.

Well, by this time my heart was whamming in my chest. I considered: God might be calling me to the Congo; but I was sure that I did not want to be a clod like Randy, who hated hamburgers and could not catch. And I did not want to live where a *mombt* could sentence me to an early death.

I rubbed my fists into my closed eyes, the way I saw adults do at their most pious, and prayed: *Most precious heavenly Father, You know I want to do Thy will, but the Congo scares me to death. Please help me to know if You are calling me there. Please don't call me there, but* . . . I ended with a Gethsemane flourish . . . *not my will but Thine.*

Then I heard Dr. Lynn say that a good way to tell if you were being called was if you felt your heart beating a little faster. Upon hearing this information, my whamming heart accelerated until I feared it would dislodge itself in some mortal way. I began to be nauseated. I tried to get hold of myself by actually getting ahold of myself; I crisscrossed and wrapped my arms around my sides and tried to squeeze myself into the resolution to remain immobile. I squeezed hard. And then the muscles along the sides of my torso took over and gave one great death-grip involuntary contraction; it felt as if my body were trying to turn inside out. I could not catch my breath. I was in terrific pain.

I rose and stumbled, trotting toward the exit. The death-grip contraction loosened, but before I could reach the outside air, an usher with the inevitable carnation in his buttonhole put his arm around me and started to walk along with me. We did not speak. I was concentrating on breathing deeply, in an effort to avoid throwing up on the sacral red carpet, and did not wonder where he was taking me.

We stepped out of the sanctuary and into one of the small offices in the education building. A man whom I recognized to be one of the deacons sat behind a gray desk. The usher left me with him.

"Why did you come forward?" he asked me. "Do you want to go to the Congo?"

"Yes," I lied.

As soon as I came back into the sanctuary and my mother took me into her arms and told me how pleased she was and my dad gave me an affectionately rough rub on the head with his knuckles, I rationalized and decided that my decision was an example of God working in mysterious ways: The involuntary contraction of my muscles, which propelled me out of my seat, was an importunate push toward my destiny by the Almighty.

My mother told me that despite tomorrow being a

school day, I would be allowed to see the Lynns off at the airport. We had to rush them there as soon as they finished shaking the last well-wisher's hand.

Dr. Lynn, Randy, and I sat in the backseat as we drove once again along the San Diego Freeway. Randy could not stop clapping his arm around me and telling me that he would be the doctor and I would be the preacher. "You really know how to tell people off," he said, kidding me. We would make the best missionary team Congo had ever seen. Randy sat between his father and me, and I was glad, because I did not want his father to think he had to counsel me concerning my decision.

Actually, during that whole half-hour car ride, Dr. Lynn never said anything to me or anyone else. His face was darkened by a five o'clock shadow (to which the night seemed to cling), and his tired eyes looked outward toward the saddleback hills. I imagined that he was thinking of the ordeals and dangers he must soon face. He had a small, bobbed nose, and with his brown hair and white skin that even the African sun could not darken, he looked childlike and strangely beaten.

We entered the airport, plunging back into its feeling of constant movement. The mechanical letters on the arrival and departure boards *chiched* away, and the walls of the corridor again resounded with the voice of the public-address announcer. We walked quickly down the corridor, and I felt a part of this event, as if *I* were about to disembark.

At the gate we stood saying good-bye. Randy insisted on kissing me on both cheeks—like the French, he said. And then, before he left, Dr. Lynn extended his hand to me, and while we shook at length, he told me that he would pray for me. It would give him great joy, he said, if he lived to see the day of my arrival on the mission field.

I watched Dr. Lynn and Randy walk to their plane. The pair of them seemed but one person, and I was that person. I knew very well that soon, quite soon, my body would enact the comic betrayal of adolescence. And I felt that one day I would be that man with the tired eyes. He seemed to be flying not to Chicago, but into a future where, watching for unknown dangers, I poled a pirogue along a silt-clouded river, the banks lined with ferns, bamboo, and the bonelike limbs of great acacia trees. And then suddenly I smelled the watery ivy and the soil and could not catch my breath, and I believed for the first time that I would die.

I do not know if, in my recurring nightmare, I see again that vision of myself as a solitary boatman. But I do know that when I awake, this curious scent of mortality lingers, as does the sense of suffocation and the certitude of death. I did not become a missionary to the Belgian Congo (now Zambia), but I did not reject the faith, either. Other religious commitments, authentic ones, and a capacity for academics I inherited from my mother led me into seminary. I am now the assistant pastor of my old home church, the First Baptist Church of San Cariño. And yet I am still as terrified of death as I was that day I first encountered it. So I come out into the living room, sit—and yes—pray.

Persecuted for Christ's Sake

BEATRICE FLINT, using all of her strength, dragged a tall-legged chair across her kitchen floor and positioned it sideways against the refrigerator. She pulled out the chair's stepladder mechanism and paused a moment to compose herself. Leaning over from the waist, she gripped the refrigerator's long, stainless-steel handle as if it were a rope she were about to climb. Then she found the first step with her slipper and, taking three handholds for every step, ascended.

Once on top, she felt dizzy. She felt as if she were flying—to her cataractal eyes the frothy, swirling pattern of the linoleum floor might have been low-lying cloud cover. She imagined herself dead on the floor, with the heavy lenses of her glasses smashed and blood running in the channels of her wrinkles. Then she thought about Emma Harris finding her in this state, and the thought so appalled Beatrice that it was as if she had inhaled a steadying draft of pure oxygen. In short order, she opened the cabinet above the refrigerator and brought the scalloped-edged punch bowl down.

Miss Emma Harris, in her official capacity as visitation

director for the First Baptist Church of San Cariño, had come to call on Beatrice every Saturday afternoon since Beatrice had moved from West Texas to California six months ago. Beatrice's younger brother, Frank, attended the church and had originally asked Emma to come. But Beatrice could not understand why Emma had returned each week with the doggedness of a debt collector. And so at noon on this Saturday, Beatrice was about to make a whiskey punch, an old-fashioned truth serum.

And yet, with the punch bowl on the counter next to the sink amid the ingredients, she was not as certain of success as she had been when the idea had come to her. Even if Emma had been telling the truth when she had said, in her self-righteous voice, that she had never touched liquor in her life, she might still be able to tell that the punch had been spiked.

Making Emma talk, however, remained Beatrice's one last wish on this earth—for all time, in fact, since she did not believe in an afterlife. Emma's piety nettled and vexed Beatrice. It questioned Beatrice's personal articles of religion, that people acted exclusively from selfish motives, that good people were simply too cowardly to be bad, that holiness was the precinct of flim-flam. She needed her suspicions confirmed that Emma was after Frank or a higher position in the church hierarchy. And yet, what if the punch prompted Emma only to repeat her claim that Christ had laid Beatrice's soul upon her heart? What then? Beatrice considered and found that she did not actually have it in her to kill the woman.

Beatrice decided to make the punch and use it or not when the time came. With her gnarled hand, she scooped the sherbet into the bowl. Then she added the ginger ale and the very light Canadian whiskey she had had the young fellow who lived across the street buy for her.

Emma Harris parked her car against the curb across the street from Miss Flint's mock-adobe bungalow. She took out her compact from her purse. Not looking directly, but obliquely, into the rearview mirror—so that she might focus a medically objective eye on a section of oily skin, rather than see the particularly unflattering reflection peculiar to rearview mirrors—she powdered her face. Then she reshaped her high, French-twist hairdo, her hands hovering in the air like those of a Hindu goddess.

After this, she looked to see that she had not spilled any of the powder on her three-piece, navy blue suit. Early in her career as visitation director, she had overheard someone at church describe her as "that respectable-looking woman in the navy blue suit." She had liked that image of herself so much that she had purchased a new navy blue suit every two years since and always wore this suit on the days when she made her calls.

She paused for a moment and prayed that she would be used of the Holy Spirit to break through Miss Flint's shell of blasphemy and pride. Then she checked her purse to see that her Soul Winner's New Testament was there. This New Testament had been a great aid to her ministry; it had a section in the back which listed appropriate Bible verses for various categories of distress, such as "For the Sick," "For Those Experiencing Temptation," "For Those Who Mourn." A pamphlet, *Faith-Full Answers*, which she had brought along especially for Miss Flint, marked the passage in the Gospel of Mark in which Christ says that those who blaspheme against the Holy Spirit are in danger of eternal damnation. She intended to discuss this passage with Miss Flint, if God granted her the opportunity.

Emma grabbed up her bag and walked across the street, but on the cement walkway of Miss Flint's home, she stopped, closed her eyes, and put her hand to her brow. Behind the left eye she felt two or three soft pulsations of pain; a migraine headache coming on. She should not let this visit upset her the way it did. She reminded herself that she should be thankful in all things and that there is a heavenly reward for those who are persecuted for Christ's sake. Quite unexpectedly, she remembered the song she used to sing as a child, about receiving a heavenly crown, and she imagined that crown—she imagined the sapphire in it that she would earn for visiting Miss Flint. Determined once more, she walked up and rang the doorbell.

Miss Flint appeared at the door, as she always did, in one of her knee-length bathrobes—today's was yellow with pink and orange flowers—and her furry, electric-blue slippers. Both the robe and the slippers drew attention to her atrophied calves. Her copper colored wig tilted to one side. She greeted Emma with the courtesy of a diplomat from a hostile nation.

They entered the living room, the shabby arena of their talks. Paintings of matadors thrusting lances into agonized, eye-rolling bulls in fluorescent colors on black velveteen hung on the turquoise walls. Magazines and weekly tabloids featuring photos of Hollywood stars, and old Spiegel catalogues, covered the mahogany furniture and most of the floor space. There were only two places in the living room where one might sit, the armchair and the rocker. Above and just to the side of the rocker hung the cage of Henry, Miss Flint's parakeet. Visitors excited Henry. Whenever Emma sat below him, he flew about his cage, his feet and wings scattering birdseed and his own dried excretions. On previous visits Miss Flint had made it clear that the rocking chair hurt her back and that she expected Emma to do "the Christian thing" and sit under Henry. So, after waiting a moment and swallowing, Emma walked over and sat in the rocking chair and smiled in a transcendent way. Henry chirped and flitted about, and his own special rain began to fall.

After Beatrice sat down, Emma said, "I saw Frank at church Sunday. He said you were having trouble with your eyes again."

"I see well enough," Beatrice said. "Sometimes I think I see more than my brother and his kind, those who are *supposed* to have 'eyes to see'—the eyes of faith."

"If you had faith," Emma said curtly, "I'm sure Christ would give you the strength to let Dr. Hall operate."

"Perhaps He'd just heal me outright and save the expense," Beatrice said and bobbed her head, once, quickly, as if to punctuate her remark.

"What would you like to talk about today? I brought some literature," Emma said, making a show of rummaging in her purse, "that I thought I might read to you." She pulled her New Testament out, with the pamphlet in it.

"A tract, you mean?"

"It's called *Faith-Full Answers,* and it gives answers to the ten questions unbelievers have most often about Christianity. It lists Bible verses which back up the answers, too." Emma put her hand on her New Testament, to show that she could supply the evidence upon demand.

"What kind of questions?"

"Well, you're always asking why Christians don't seem to be better than anybody else."

"Better?" Beatrice said. "They're *worse* most of the time. Did I tell you about the preacher I knew in Longview, Texas, who got this girl in the family way and told her she couldn't tell no one because the baby was a gift of the Holy Spirit? That girl tried to give birth out in a cow shed like some Virgin Mary, and they didn't find her for two days. She only had time to tell on the preacher before she died."

"Yes," Emma said in a strangely agreeable voice, "I think you did mention that incident, once."

"It bears repeating, don't you think?"

"I doubt that man was a true servant of the Lord."

"That man was no better than an animal."

"But Christ came to save sinners like that man, Beatrice. You see," Emma said, opening the pamphlet, "it says here that Christians are not any better than anyone else. They have simply acknowledged their unworthiness in the sight of Almighty God and have been forgiven."

"When I was a little girl in Sunday school, they used to say, 'By their fruits ye shall know them.' As far as I can see, the Christians in this world are dying of the scurvy."

"And the devil can quote Scripture for his purpose."

Emma smiled, trying to mitigate the implication of her remark.

Beatrice made a clucking noise with her tongue against the roof of her palate and puckered her lips, as if she tasted a very bitter substance indeed.

They waited for a time, long enough for Emma to feel wrapped, clothed, in the quiet. Then Beatrice said, "The talk's made me dry. I've made some punch. It's all made—you just sit, and I'll carry it out."

Emma would normally have offered to help, but she needed the time to collect her thoughts. Each week she had tried to come up with an irrefutable argument—an article of the faith which had to be accepted, something which would admit no further discussion—on the basis of which she might convince Beatrice that she needed to attend the church. Today, if the pamphlet did not work, Emma had decided to confront Beatrice with death and damnation.

But now that she had already numbered Beatrice among Lucifer's minions, the old woman's anger blazed more brightly than any vision of hell Emma might conjure. She felt hopeless: For one of the few times in her twenty-year ministry, she wanted to escape, to walk quietly out the door while Beatrice was still in the kitchen.

The soft pulsations of pain behind her left eye suddenly became stabs. Soon her migraine would transform her skull into a private torture chamber; she would hold her head in her shaking hands and frantically massage her scalp, as if she might tear it open and thereby release the pain. She calculated that it was a five-mile drive from Beatrice's house to hers: If she drank a glass of punch and quickly excused herself, she would be home before her headache tablets made her too dizzy to drive. So she found the prescription bottle she always carried with her in her black leather bag and shook two codeine tablets into her hand.

Beatrice carried in the punch bowl and set it on the table against the far wall. Then she brought in two cut-crystal cups and filled them. She handed Emma her glass, along with a napkin which had printing on it that read "Happy New Year!" and a drawing of people in party hats throwing streamers and blowing toy horns at one another.

Emma put the two small, round tablets into her mouth and drained her punch, so that the tablets would not lodge in her throat. She noticed Beatrice watching her. Beatrice's gauzy look of half-blindness suddenly cleared, becoming a frank stare. Emma thought Beatrice felt insulted that she had not bothered to taste what Beatrice had laboriously prepared. So Emma quickly asked for another glass.

"You feeling all right, Miss Harris?" Beatrice asked as she ladled out another cup for Emma.

"I get these headaches sometimes. When I'm tired. It's nothing, really."

"Frank used to get headaches like that," Beatrice said. "They gave him pills. Have they given you pills? Frank's a chemist, you know. He asked the pharmacist what those pills were and found out that they were nothing more than glorified aspirin. So he told the pharmacist no thank-you and went out and bought him some aspirin—not even brand name—and that worked just fine."

Emma listened without hearing and sipped her second glass of punch. The beverage was rich and heavy and possessed an unusual tang; it made the sherbet taste especially soothing. She found that once she had become accustomed to the taste, she liked the way it cooled her breath like an after-dinner mint.

"I suppose," Beatrice said, "your ministry must be a great burden to you. I suppose that's why you get these headaches."

Emma looked at Beatrice, trying to divine what stratagem this newfound concern concealed. But Beatrice's long, narrow face, made even longer and more narrow by its sagging into a double chin, betrayed nothing. Behind her gaze, sphinxlike and blind once more, she waited with timeless patience for an answer.

"My ministry," Emma said, "is a great comfort to me. I don't know what I would have done with my life if the Lord hadn't given me this work."

"You've been at it quite a while, then."

"Since 1953."

"How do you know who to call on? People at the church give you names, I suppose. Like Frank did."

Emma nodded.

"Would you like some more punch?" Beatrice asked.

Emma thought that she might stay for five more minutes. She usually did not feel light-headed or experience any of the spatial distortion the pills brought on for forty-five minutes. "Thank-you, Miss Flint. I believe I will."

While drinking her punch, Emma noted that her headache was abating and that her body felt comfortably lethargic, a bit slow to react. That Beatrice now asked about her life, coupled with her making this punch, suggested that she had planned a reconciliation of sorts, to ask Emma's forgiveness for her past behavior through these gestures. That story about the Longview preacher had been a reflex reaction. Emma resolved to wait until the last minute to leave.

"Does everyone cause you the bother I do?" Beatrice asked, and her face took on a childlike simplicity—it said that there really could be no secrets between them.

Emma almost replied with an offhand protest, but then thought better of it. "You've been a challenge, old girl." She did not know why she had used this appellation—it had very much "slipped out"—but one look at Beatrice assured Emma that the old woman had not taken offense; indeed, she was smiling with a strange satisfaction. "But mainly I've enjoyed our visits. We've talked. We've discussed your questions. Other times, I've gotten into real situations, I'll tell you."

"Well, tell me, then."

"The most embarrassing is when you get in the midst of domestic quarrels. This one time," Emma said, putting her hand to her mouth in an attempt to stifle a laugh which issued anyway in short, nasal wheezes. "This one time these two were so busy making up that I had to let myself out." She paused, remembered that house and how she had lingered, heard the door close, and then soft, muffled sounds. "That was fine, though. So nice. What were we talking about?"

"The hard places you've gotten into."

"The people I really dread, you know, are the Jehovah's Witnesses. I'll give them a piece of literature and then they'll tell me to wait. When they come to the door again, they've got a *Watchtower* in their hand, and they start talking about calling God by His right name. I can't even bring myself to talk with them anymore. I turn right around, shake the dust off my feet—as it says to do in the Bible—remind myself that it's a privilege to be persecuted for Christ's sake, and walk on."

"I'm disappointed," Beatrice said. "I would have thought I'd be worth three Witnesses."

At that moment, with her wig askew atop her wizened head, Beatrice appeared, to Emma, the image of a kindly old grandmother. Her sloppiness, her lack of taste, her sharp tongue were all transformed into endearing idiosyncrasies. Emma felt sorry for the enmity that had existed between them. Though she realized this was absurd, she longed to cross the distance between them and wrap her arms around the old woman's neck and cry away their collective sorrows.

"But those people," Beatrice said. "You meet up with them just once. You call on me every week. It perplexes me why you keep at it. Does Frank ask you to come?"

"He suggested it, yes." An interior voice warned her to be cautious. She usually attended to this voice, but at that moment it had lost all of its sober resonance, becoming instead a high-pitched, comic squeal. Emma sat within a profound peace, which seemed to have spread through her body down into her limbs.

"So you do it for him—for Frank?" Beatrice asked.

Emma looked up at Beatrice, and the more Emma tried to focus on the old woman, the farther away Beatrice seemed to be. Emma asked Beatrice to repeat herself. She did.

"I visit anyone I'm asked to visit."

"But what I mean is," Beatrice said, "are you always so dedicated, like you've been with me?"

"I don't understand."

"Listen, girl, I've been trying to figure you out, and I can't. I've been wondering if there's anything special about me or about Frank that would make you come back time after time the way you do."

The feeling of peace in which Emma's body had luxuriated now congealed, hardened into fear-ridden self-absorption. She felt isolated and small in her rocking chair.

"What do you think of Frank?" Beatrice asked, her voice flat and direct.

"He's a fine . . . ," and here Emma burped and knew from the way her stomach rolled and clenched that a terrible uneasiness was brewing there.

"What do think of Frank?"

"He's a fine Christian man."

"Don't you think more of him than just that he's a fine man?" Beatrice's voice softened, became knowing, conspiratorial. "You think *the world* of him, don't you Emma?"

Caught, pinned, Emma recognized the truth of what Beatrice said. But even more, she knew—through the shame, embarrassment, and humiliation she felt—that this truth exposed others which she had for so long tried to conceal, not from others so much as from herself. She also knew that she was about to be uncontrollably ill. In her confused state, with Beatrice and the table and the stacks of movie magazines rearranging their proximity to her, the atmosphere pervaded by a yellow light into which objects seemed to dissolve and then reappear, she felt that Beatrice's intuition of her motives had caused this external display of her internal confusion.

A moment later, the room still being thrown about crazily by her private poltergeists, her mouth started to water. She attempted to move, but could not—not even enough to hang her head to one side when the eruption came. The vomit was hot and full in her throat. It came out of her nose as well as her mouth. It was so sickeningly cloying that the aftertaste occasioned several repetitions. Her blue suit was covered with the syrupy ooze. She cried softly and moaned, a sound of profound regret and abandonment. Henry, the bird, went berserk in his cage.

Then Beatrice was at her side. She asked Emma if she felt well enough to go into the bathroom. Emma held her head in her hands and took several deep breaths. She rested another moment—rested until she determined that throwing up had rendered the world stable once more. Beatrice guided Emma into the bathroom and told her to take off her clothes, she would give her something to put on and then clean Emma's clothes as best she could. But Emma insisted on attending to her blue suit herself.

Stripped down to her foundation garments, Emma stood at the sink. Though she could barely control her hands, she took a wet washcloth and wiped the trails and spatterings of lime green effusion off each piece of her suit. In the course of this washing, the suit became thoroughly soaked—other sections of the material passed under the running faucet while she worked on the stained areas. Finally, defeated, she hung the suit over the side of the bathtub.

She looked into the mirror over the sink, smoothing

back the wet, matted hair from her forehead and staring directly at herself. She forced herself to look at her oily, pockmarked skin, at her long, fleshy, now swollen nose, and at her almond-shaped eyes, which had been transformed into multilegged insects by running mascara. Emma still felt the shame of her unworthy motives. Somehow she wished to cauterize the source of that shame by truly, radically, facing herself—to lance the wound of what she now recognized as her vanity.

Emma heard the shuffling of Beatrice's slippers outside in the hall. The door partially opened and the old woman's slack-skinned arm extended one of her quilted bathrobes, a robe patterned with large, American Beauty roses. Emma took it, told Beatrice she would be out in a few minutes, and shut the door again. With her two hands at the robe's shoulders, she held the garment out before her. It represented everything about Beatrice's life that Emma feared; it was the twilight world in which the old woman lived, alone, adorned not for any visitor except death. Emma felt she could not stand to put the robe on, but when she looked back to her blue suit, she found it to be wet, misshaped, malodorous—she would probably never be able to wear it again. And so, with a resignation that bespoke the irreversible, she put on the bathrobe.

Emma went out to the living room then, where she found Beatrice sitting in the rocking chair. There were dark circles on the hooked rug by the chair, where Beatrice must have cleaned. Sitting in the armchair, Emma observed Beatrice. The old woman appeared agitated; she rocked violently in the chair, turned her head from side to side—never looking at Emma—and muttered to herself.

"My clothes," Emma said, "won't dry for some time, I'm afraid. Shall we put them out on the clothesline in back?"

"I just couldn't stand it anymore, that's all," Beatrice said. "You told me you never drank, but how was I to know you'd be allergic? I made the punch mild. I wanted to loosen your tongue, not unhinge your insides."

Emma had not even thought about a physical, external cause for her sickness. She considered explaining to Beatrice about her codeine tablets, but that was not what she wanted to tell the old woman now. So she simply said, "I'm fine, Beatrice. Even if it had to come out that way, I'm glad we know about Frank."

"As I said," Beatrice replied, and halted her rocking before continuing in a dignified, judicious voice, "I see well enough. I knew there had to be something going on. No one wants to come calling on a blind old bat like me." Beatrice bobbed her head, punctuating, and then leaned back in the rocker and smiled slyly.

"You did see," Emma admitted. "But not everything, I think. When I was a girl of seven, my uncle and aunt came to visit my parents. They were still at the table after dinner when I came into the kitchen. I could hear their voices through the swinging door between the two rooms. My oldest sister was about to be married. My father jokingly complained about having to pay for our weddings—there were four of us girls—I was the youngest. And then my aunt said, she said, 'Emma won't cost you a penny. That's one ugly duck that will *never* turn into a swan.' And my parents laughed. Not in a polite way, but as if they were relieved, as if I embarrassed them so much that they were relieved to have me be nothing but the butt of a joke. What my aunt said was like a prophecy. I grew up knowing what she said was true, seeing it everyday in the mirror. All the time the one thing I feared was that I would be . . . an old maid." Emma looked down, her cheeks flushed.

"Go on, girl," Beatrice said. "You can say *old maid*—it doesn't bother me. I never married, but I had my men—and on my own terms, too. Go on, now."

"When the pastor came to me and asked me to be the visitation director, it seemed to me that God was delivering me. I thought if I worked hard enough at it, God would have to reward me. He would lead me to the right man. But then I got older and I kept visiting these families, having it thrown up in my face all the time. So I tried to forget about it, to think about the good I was doing. But I couldn't. All I wanted was for a man to be behind the next door—even a married man—anybody who would love me. That's all I wanted." She began to cry in a gentle, quiet way. Beatrice handed Emma a tissue, and she blew her fleshy, swollen nose.

"And then Frank," Emma said, and sniffled. "I thought if I brought you to church, he would be grateful and take an interest. I'm sorry. That's all I can say."

"Well, pshaw, girl. If you'd have told me, I would have let you carry me to church. I don't mind you trying to interest Frank—if you're fool enough to want him." She paused and then said, "I should tell you, though, Frank claims he won't remarry unless his eyes go bad like mine and he loses his driver's license."

Emma laughed: a laugh which gathered into it the misery of her life and reduced that misery to the poignant sound of laughter and then to silence and then to nothing. It was all right if God made her into an old woman like Beatrice, rocking away toward death in an old bathrobe. She knew that God was and would always be her lover.

They sat for a time in silence and then went to see about Emma's clothes. Her blue suit had barely dried at all. Emma decided to drive home in Beatrice's bathrobe and promised to return it when she paid Beatrice her usual visit the next Saturday.

Palm Sunday

IT WAS PALM SUNDAY at the First Baptist Church of San Cariño. Six arrangements of towering palms, sprouting out of white wicker baskets, stood before the sanctuary's platform, celebrating Jesus' triumphal entry into Jerusalem. Members of the congregation, waiting for the service to begin, exchanged greetings and pleasantries in suppressed, breathy voices; the noise of the many conversations filled the sanctuary and created an atmosphere of expectancy.

Sam Anderson sat in the third pew from the front on the left-hand aisle next to his daughter, who was an imbecile. She was not an imbecile in the sense that she had made a mess and caused an argument at the breakfast table that morning (although she had); she was an imbecile in the technical sense of the word: Her mental age would never surpass five, and she would require lifelong supervision in the performance of the routine daily tasks of caring for herself.

Sam's position in the sanctuary on this Sunday morning was strategic. He was close enough to the platform and the choir loft that his daughter might be distracted by the progressive events of the worship service. His daughter lacked even the short attention span of most ten-year-old children; she did, however, have a peculiar tendency to be hypnotized by sheer motion. If she was placed very close to the platform, the preacher, Reverend March—who was given to a strutting, gesturing style of oration—kept her attention for remarkably long periods of time. Sam was also close to the front side exit, which led into the education building, in case he had to take his daughter out.

His daughter had not been seated more than a minute before she became restless. She started to crawl on the floor between the pews, away from Sam. The image of an old sow rooting along in a trough came to his mind. He quickly grabbed hold of the back of her pink dress and stopped her. She turned and with surprising quickness scrambled up and sat in his lap. She took the lapels of his suit jacket in her hands and nuzzled her head against his chest. Tired of nuzzling, she began thumping her head against his chest, pushing him away with her hands and bringing her head into him again and again.

Though only ten, his daughter was over five feet tall and weighed one hundred and thirty-three pounds, so that her presence in his lap made him uncomfortable; the head thumping was painful—she possessed almost inhuman strength.

He reached into the brown lunch bag by his side and gave his daughter Dolly. Dolly was an old, naked doll with a strangely sophisticated plastic face and a rubbery body which had babylike rings of fat at the joints of the limbs. She was the constant companion of his daughter. The girl had to be tricked into letting the toy out of her sight, so that it might be magically produced at moments like this. With Dolly in her arms, Sam was able to push her off his lap onto the pew. His daughter sat enraptured; she bathed the doll's face in kisses with her red fish lips and then sat sucking the doll's foot.

Sam looked at his daughter and thought again of the sow. He had been on a farm exactly twice in his life, and yet these barnyard images, though they were unbidden, unwelcome, came to mind. She was a mule, an ox, a pig—any animal—but not human. If man was a marriage of the divine and the beastly, then nature had conspired to make his offspring an exemplar of man's lower nature. It was not enough that her mental capacity had to be so limited, her body must attest to this fact. Everything about his daughter, her large, somehow formless shape, her features—little saucer eyes, a pug nose, and those fish lips—which were lost in her great moon face, her wispy strawberry blond hair, as thin and scarce as a toddler's, spoke of the flesh encroaching on the spirit.

Other parents of children like his own, whose stories he had read in *Reader's Digest* and other magazines, spoke of how their children kept them alert to sensations and feelings, to elemental expressions of love, which in their simple purity were unmistakably genuine. All of this was probably true, but could as well be said of a dog as of a retarded child. These parents often spoke, too, of an overpowering love for the retarded child, which came to them despite their initial resistance, even repulsion. Sam had received no such revelation of charity.

The service began. The young assistant pastor, Michael Dennis, welcomed the congregation to the Palm Sunday worship service and made the announcements. Then it was time to sing a hymn, "All Glory, Laud and Honor." The congregation rose to its feet. Sam's daughter sat, opening and closing one of Dolly's plastic eyelids with a pudgy finger. But when the congregation began to sing, she stood up. She made no sound during the first verse, but rocked back and forth, swaying with the languorous lines. On the second verse she began to hum in her own way, between her teeth, tunelessly, fervently—the sound of a man in such distress that he has given up calling for help and has begun his own arrhythmic, moaning dirge. The volume of this moaning increased, being particularly noticeable in the breath pauses and those between verses. It was quite useless for Sam to put his finger before his mouth and signal for his daughter to be quiet; music moved her powerfully.

Long ago he had learned that the only way to quiet her was to resort to a signal his wife and he had used when his daughter was very young. For a very long time she had not been able to respond to even the rudiments of language: *yes* and *no* meant nothing to her. She could only be coerced into behaving in a particular way by direct physical signals. Trying to teach her that when they shook they heads back and forth they meant no, they had shaken their daughter's head. Eventually, she had learned that when they shook her head, she was to stop whatever she was doing.

So now, during the hymn singing, Sam took his daughter's head in the crook of his arm, put a gentle hammerlock on her, and forcefully jiggled. The signal worked only to a certain extent. Clasping his daughter to his chest, he endured the rest of the hymn, prayed that she would quit moaning when the last verse was sung, and wondered why he should commit himself to the practiced agony of bringing his daughter to church. That was the question his wife had posed that morning, the issue

over which they had had an argument after his daughter
had dumped her Cheerios onto the breakfast table.

Sam was not, in the ordinary sense, a religious man.
He knew that his wife was an unbeliever and was training their normal son in her skeptical ways, and Sam
made no significant protest. Before his daughter was
born, he attended and enjoyed services because he had
grown up attending church. The Gospel, which was to
him nothing if not an old, old story, reassured him; it was
the half-remembered poetry from childhood, in terms of
which he hoped always to see life.

But then when his daughter had been born, his moti-
vation changed. He did not attend at all for the first five
years of her life; these last five years he had not missed a
Sunday, except for vacations. He supposed, though he
had not told his wife this that morning, and would never
tell her or anyone, that he was presenting his daughter to
God. This presentation was in essence an accusation: He
wanted God to take notice of what He had done, and
Sam wanted, if not an apology, at least an answer to the
question she posed.

If Sam had told his wife about this matter, had tried to
explain what question the child posed, he would have
had to remind his wife about how their daughter
scratched her head, tapped her toe, and hitched her
pants. His daughter performed these mannerisms in
exactly the way and on precisely those occasions when
he did. Most parents see in their children's mimicry an
image of eternity, and divine from this image reason to
believe that even the most transitory gesture receives its
meaning from an unknown but half-guessed relation to
the timeless. Their faith in life rises. His daughter's

mimicry had the opposite effect; it made him despair. It seemed to be the *reductio ad absurdum* of his way of being in the world. It made of his life a Punch and Judy show that he could not be comfortable with or affirm in the old way.

After the song ended, Sam was able to revive his daughter's interest in Dolly. She played with the toy on the pew and on the floor at Sam's feet until Reverend March began to preach. She insisted, then, on climbing back into Sam's lap and would not be budged. She did, however, keep reasonably still and quiet during the course of the sermon.

Appropriately enough, Reverend March preached that day on the Palm Sunday event, Jesus' triumphal entry into Jerusalem. His theme was the recognition of Christ. He wondered aloud, building suspense through drawing out his argument, how the people of Jerusalem could have recognized Jesus as the Messiah on this Sunday and then five days hence have crucified Him. They saw Him one day for who He was, and then in five days they mistook Him for a criminal, one worthy of capital punishment.

"But then," Reverend March asked, "isn't that like people today? Don't we see Christ and recognize Him as Lord one day and then turn our backs on Him the next? Of course, we don't actually have the person of Jesus walking around in our midst. Or do we? Isn't the church the body of Christ? Don't we see Christ in the church at times, but fail to recognize Him at others? But Christ is always here, here in the lives of other people. Our inability to see Christ in others is often due to our inability to see Christ in our own lives.

"Whose fault can that be? Not the Lord's. He is always available, always beseeching us to come into communion with Him. Will you come into communion with Christ today, recognize Him as those along the road into Jerusalem recognized Him that day two thousand years ago?"

Then Reverend March explained that in a moment he would pray and after that they would sing the invitation hymn, and all those who wanted to recognize Christ, to accept Him as Lord and Saviour, or who wanted to find out more about doing so, were to come forward and meet with trained counsellors who were ready to talk and pray about these matters.

Reverend March prayed. Sam looked at his daughter, watching for signs of the peculiar state into which she had fallen during the altar call for the last several weeks. Still sitting on his now numb lap, she had folded her hands for the prayer, though her saucer eyes remained opened. She made no sound, yet.

The invitation hymn was chiefly responsible for the state into which she fell, Sam thought. His daughter did not respond to the invitation hymn as she responded to the other hymns, with her own brand of singing. The invitation hymn, at least for the past three weeks, had caused her to whine like a dog and to roll her head from side to side on the back of the pew in front of them. He had not taken her out because of the noise; her whining was soft, feeble. The invitation hymn, with its slow cadences and swelling melodies, produced in his daughter a state of emotional distress—her face became a mottled red, and she squeezed her eyes shut as if resisting pain.

When he had taken her out in the past, she had begun

to cry in earnest—long, homesick wails. For the better part of an hour he had had to walk her around in the parking lot before she calmed down enough for him to take her home. The experience made him question whether he should bring her to the services at all. If services were a somehow necessary agony for him, they had proved a painful bewilderment to his daughter. Why not be content with teaching his daughter to recite. "God is great, God is good, let us thank Him for our food," and be content knowing that he had taught her all of the "religious poetry" that she would ever be able to understand? And yet, she would be with him for such a short while now: His wife insisted that as soon as his daughter started to menstruate, she be institutionalized. The way she was growing, that would be very soon. He did not know what to do. He sat and waited for what would happen next.

At Reverend March's command, the congregation stood and began to sing the invitation hymn, "Coming Home." His daughter got off Sam's lap and stood by him. The refrain concluded the first verse:

Coming home, coming home, never more to roam
Open wide thine arms of love, Lord I'm coming home.

On the second verse, the whimpering and whining began. Only this time, his daughter did not bend over and press her forehead to the pew before them. This time she bounced a bit on her feet, pranced almost, and swung her head forward and back. Another barnyard image: She reminded him of a horse tied up but ready to bolt. She was going wild; it was extraordinary. He took her hand firmly and began to lead her out.

As soon as they reached the aisle, she did bolt; she escaped his grasp and ran, her arms and legs churning. He did not follow; at that moment he was overcome with embarrassment that she was his own. She grabbed one of the palms from a wicker basket, a great many-fingered fan as tall as she, and headed up the platform steps. Sam looked to see what Reverend March would do, but the pastor did not see the child on the platform. His attention was directed to a woman and young boy, mother and son from their appearance, who were coming forward in response to the invitation.

Then Sam's daughter began to wail, issuing unearthly ululations, piercing howls that were not plaintive, but discernibly joyful. She swung the palm about her head in great circles and howled and howled. There was something primitive about it. Sam thought of the movie he had seen of tribal rites, in which a man in an elaborate headdress that made him look like a gigantic bird, danced in circles. Sam looked at Reverend March, who looked back this time. Then they both looked alternately at his daughter and at the young mother and son who were coming forward. The organist, trying to cover the child's howls, immediately began the third verse after the second.

Reverend March walked over to where Sam's daughter stood on the platform, offered her his hand, which she took, and led her over to the pulpit. She stopped howling, but she kept a grip on her palm with her free hand and occasionally whirled it around, the pointed leaves just missing Reverend March's head. The pastor then signalled for the organist to stop playing after the third verse and gestured for Sam to join them on the stage. Sam walked forward, looking about him as if asking the crowd for permission to appear on the platform. Soon he was beside his daughter, with the rows of faces before him.

"People," Reverend March said, "there are two kinds of understanding: the understanding of the head and the understanding of the heart. Sometimes we hear things and we believe them, but the knowledge doesn't really penetrate our hearts, our souls. At times, I *preach* on subjects without having what one might call a 'soulful understanding.' Today I did. But this girl has shown me—has shown us all—that Christ has indeed come into our midst today. He has made a triumphal entry into our congregation through the lives of the two people who have come forward. We should lift our voices and cry out, as this girl has been crying out, 'Hosanna! Blessed is He that cometh in the name of the Lord.' Let's try it one time. Repeat after me. 'Hosanna!' "

"Hosanna," the crowd responded.

"Louder now. Hosanna!"

"Hosanna!"

"Hosanna!"

"HOSANNA."

His daughter began to howl again, but Sam saw that Reverend March and the congregation regarded her with affection. She seemed to know this and delight in it.

Reverend March leaned over to Sam and asked, "What's your daughter's name, again?"

"Cynthia." Sam loved the name Cynthia, and when he had been informed that his daughter was severely retarded, he had been sorry he had wasted the name on her. He had stopped thinking of her as Cynthia. But now

he was quite suddenly and overwhelmingly glad he had
named her as he had.

"Let's all say it together with Cynthia," Reverend
March said. "Three times, when I raise my hand."

"HOSANNA!"

"HOSANNA!"

"HOSANNA!"

Mrs. Sunday's Problem

MRS. WILL (SHORT FOR WILFRED) WHITE SUNDAY might be said to have been a member, if such a class exists at all, of the American evangelical aristocracy. Her forebears had found the Lord in a New England town during the Great Awakening. Since then, every branch of the White family had produced prominent churchmen. In the past two generations her grandfather had been a Baptist minister, her great-aunt and -uncle part of the China mission, and her father taught apologetics and homiletics in a seminary and practiced the latter in neighboring churches on Sundays. Her husband's family was distantly related to Billy Sunday, the baseball player who became a combative evangelist.

Mrs. Sunday met Daniel, her husband, at Wheaton College in Wheaton, Illinois, the Harvard of the evangelical aristocracy. They married soon after graduation. Mrs. Sunday, or Will, as her family called her, worked as a secretary while Daniel attended the Wharton School of Finance in Philadelphia. Their life thereafter fulfilled their upwardly mobile expectations.

If Will's life followed a predictable course, fulfilled an almost preordained pattern, that is not to say that it was unremarkable. Her ability to fulfill her family's and her own expectations without ever faltering was in itself a feat. But also, Will was one of those women who, while holding fast to the idea that a woman's chief happiness will always be found within family and domestic life, accomplishes much outside her home. Friends of Will unanimously thought of her as a "superwoman." A faultless wife and mother, a tasteful home decorator, a gourmet cook, an immaculate housekeeper, Will at the same time ran the Christian-education department at the First Baptist Church of San Cariño. She supervised all the Sunday-school departments, from the nursery through grammar school. Under her direction a staff of sixty cared for and taught Sunday-school lessons to an average weekly attendance of three hundred and eighty pupils.

More than these facts, Will's sensibility recommended her as someone whom it was a privilege to know. She was one of those rare individuals who manages to be pleasantly and discreetly virtuous. She was, in the very best sense, deeply religious, and growing up in a household of theological discussion, she enjoyed talking about her beliefs. But when she did so, her wit showed itself as well as her knowledge; after talking with Will, the most strident atheist would probably go away mysteriously troubled that his own beliefs could not quite account for such a likeable woman.

On a Wednesday morning Will stood by her car in the parking lot of her daughter, Karen's, nursery school and experienced a strange moment of misgiving. It was as if her mind had lost its moorings for a moment, and she could not orient herself in space and time; the support of knowing who and where she was—the undergirding experience of selfhood, which must be as regular as one's heartbeat—had been suddenly withdrawn, lost in a vacuous sea. But then, buoylike, her ego righted itself, floated back to the surface, and she was again the woman who belonged to this casual scene. She looked toward the windowed side of the school. The long, one-story building lay in the volatile quiet of all schools packed with unheard children. It was a fine February day; a steady breeze out of the east had blown away the smog from the valley in Los Angeles, where she lived. She could see the encircling mountains in all of their blue, primordial beauty; the sinuous folds of the ravines partitioned the range into so many fingers of God.

Will drove away from the school toward the First Baptist Church of San Cariño, where she worked as the educational director. Today there was to be a staff meeting. Will looked forward to it—attendance was up. Besides, Will especially liked these early morning planning sessions. As she drove along she imagined the staff seated around the long, cafeteria-style table, each member huddled over his cup of coffee. She could taste the coffee: strong, bitter, sweet, the taste of work itself. She reminded herself not to become too enthusiastic about her ideas, not to dominate the conversation—last week, the choir director had muttered about "equal time."

When she was several blocks from the church, on a wide four-lane boulevard, she experienced another moment of misgiving. She looked away from the road for a moment, and when she looked back, she saw a stop light ahead. Misgiving became indecision, a feeling of lethargy suffused her limbs. For unknown reasons she decided to coast and wait to see if the light would turn green. But, as if the car had taken a quantum jump, she found herself suddenly at the throat of the intersection. She tried to brake, but the feeling of lethargy in her legs congealed, became a paralysis; it was not as if she merely lacked the power to move her legs, all feeling that her legs existed ceased. At the intersection she looked at the speedometer and saw that her car was still going about twenty miles per hour. Then a car passed before her, and she screamed as she had never screamed in her life. At that instant in the middle of the intersection, she knew that her legs were dead and that if she was not killed within the next millisecond by a passing car, she would be dead anyway moments later.

Instead of dying, she went into a state in which her body performed the actions necessary to pull the car over to the curb and stop it. Her conscious mind slept, blanked out, effaced itself in such a way that she had no recollection as to how she stopped the car when she found herself at rest and safe. Before doing anything else, she looked down and watched herself move her legs in a bicycle-like motion in the constricted space beneath the steering wheel. Satisfied but still wary, she slipped off her low-heeled pumps and wiggled the toes on her stocking-clad feet.

She left the car, walked back to the intersection, and used the phone in the booth at the gasoline station on the corner. Still very much shaken, she could not recall the church's telephone number. She asked a quizzical operator to connect her, answered the operator's questions by saying that the pay phone's dial was out of order, and finally reached Michael Dennis, the church's young assistant pastor. He agreed to walk over and drive her home. She went back to the car and waited and started wondering what illness had brought on the momentary paralysis. Would it kill her, or worse, render her completely dependent? Would she have the courage to live such a life?

That afternoon she went to see her doctor. During the next week, in his office and during a two-day stay at the local Presbyterian hospital, he and his colleagues performed a battery of tests. Never once did they say what they were testing for, but the extensiveness of their probings kept Will extremely nervous and agitated. At the end of the tests the doctor had Will come to his office. He showed her into the room where he counselled patients.

The counselling room was decorated simply and in a somewhat typical manner. Her doctor, Dr. Leach, sat behind a large, walnut desk on which stood pictures of his family. On the walls hung his diplomas and paintings representing scenes from medical history: Harvey demonstrating the circulation of the blood, Roentgen with the first X-ray machine.

Dr. Leach was a bald, thin man with soft features and a paternal manner. Will liked him, but sometimes found his fatherly way condescending. He said nothing at first, but put up two X-rays on the small lighted viewer attached to the wall. She prepared herself, struggled to control her panic, but then he said that they had found nothing wrong. He showed her, in X-ray after X-ray, that nothing was wrong. She was relieved and did not pay much attention to what he was saying, until he began a transparent line of questioning about her marriage.

"You think this might be psychosomatic?" Will asked.

"We can't find any pathological cause, anything physical, that might explain it."

She felt like telling him that she knew the meaning of *pathological*, but she refrained. "Dr. Leach," she said, "you know me. Do you really think I'm some sort of Freudian detective case walking around waiting to be solved?"

"Will, you've gone through a difficult series of tests, and you were terrific. Why not go through one more test—an utterly painless one—just to make sure?"

"See a psychiatrist?"

"Why should you resist seeing one?"

"I'm not," she said somewhat petulantly. "I just wonder if it's necessary. I'll feel foolish."

"Here. I'll write the name down for you. Something did happen, Will. We ought to know all we can about it."

"Always the wise old doctor, aren't you?"

"I try to be."

Will delayed seeing a psychiatrist. She assigned the question as to what had caused her momentary paralysis to the outermost limbo of her mind, where she put all unanswered and perhaps unanswerable questions. For two weeks she took up her tasks again as mother and working woman and, except for several moments of keen self-doubt, functioned normally.

Thursday afternoon of the second week she had to give her bimonthly tea for her three age-group supervisors: Mrs. Williams, who headed the cradle roll and nursery departments, Mrs. Carol, the primary-age group supervisor, and Mrs. Jeffers, who handled the juniors. The women actually did very little business at the teas; they casually discussed curriculum and whether their departments were adequately staffed, but Will principally used the time to encourage them. The women did a substantial amount of work on a volunteer basis, and the teas were one of their job's few compensations. While providing the women with afternoons out, they also, through the guise of being business meetings, certified the importance of their work.

On these occasions, Will, as boss and hostess, maintained an attitude of beneficent authority, playing the grand yet humble lady. She found the role fatiguing and was usually a little depressed after the teas ended; her impulse was to be more businesslike; she did not like gossipy social occasions, but she knew how much she owed the women and labored to fulfill their expectations.

After she had poured several cups of tea for each woman, and the plates of little sandwiches—cream cheese mixed with carrot shavings and raisins, tuna salad on pumpernickel wedges, and watercress inside buttered cones of white bread—were nearly cleaned, the women sat in a semicircle in Will's living room and discussed the spring curriculum and the special events surrounding Easter.

Mrs. Jeffers, the most opinionated of Will's coworkers, a horsy-looking woman with large, gray eyes, wondered aloud if anyone else was upset about the cancellation of the canned-food drive. The canned-food drive had been a traditional part of the Easter season in the church since *her* days in Sunday school. Will explained again that the boarding school for handicapped children to which they gave the food had been swamped with cans at Christmas and had requested that no more food be given this year. Mrs. Jeffers still thought it a shame; the drive taught the children to share and involved the parents in the Sunday school through their gifts. Will thought about saying that if Mrs. Jeffers could raise the money required and work out the logistics of shipping the goods overseas, they could send the supplies to missionaries. But she said nothing. She excused herself, took up the sandwich tray, muttered about not letting anyone go hungry (an unintentional footnote to the canned-goods discussion), and went into the kitchen.

There in the kitchen, at her sideboard next to the electric stove, she cut more pumpernickel wedges. She spread tuna salad on them and wasted a substantial amount of time trying to arrange the wedges into a perfect circle. The ladies would soon stop talking among themselves and wonder what she was doing. She needed to think of another discussion topic before she went back into the living room.

Her thoughts, however, became as solid and nondescript as granite. Trying to think, she felt herself falling into that state of misgiving and self-doubt that she first knew outside Karen's nursery school. She felt like sitting down but was afraid that she would not be able to stand up, that the paralysis would come on again. She rested her weight on her hands at the sideboard and noticed that her hands were swollen. They had puffed up as if from an allergic reaction to bee stings.

The granitelike heaviness of her mind suddenly dissolved, gave way to liquid fear. Adrenalin shot into her

bloodstream, and her heart raced. She could not understand what she was afraid of. She could not believe that
she was terrified of her friends. She determined that she
would go into the living room, explain that she was ill,
and walk through into her bedroom. She took one step,
her knees buckled, and she fell.

Will managed to turn herself over and sit with her
arms around her knees before her co-workers ran in.
They asked what had happened, if she was all right, if
she was hurt, if she had broken anything. Mrs. Jeffers
asked if she was pregnant. Once they ascertained that
she was not injured, they expressed their collective
mothering instinct: their hands were all about her, like
waving seaweed, feeling her forehead, taking her pulse,
massaging her back, taking off her shoes. She wanted to
scream but found herself crying meekly and hated herself for it. She wanted nothing except for this scene to be
over. But she knew it would be a very long time before
they left.

The next day Will called her doctor and made an appointment with a psychiatrist, Dr. R. J. Melford. At her
first appointment on Tuesday of the following week, he
administered several tests, one of which was similar to
the personality profile given to her during Freshman
Week at her college. Two days later she returned for her
first therapy session.

Dr. Melford's office was spacious enough to make Will
feel lost and self-conscious upon entering. The back wall
behind the desk was covered with bookshelves filled
with medical tomes. A light golden brown wallpaper
covered the other three pictureless walls. A couch lined

one wall and an armchair, covered with the same chocolate brown fabric, sat on the other side of the room. This was recognizably a doctor's office, stripped of the instruments and other paraphernalia of the internist but with the same feeling for proportion and order, homeostasis. Dr. Melford, leafing through papers on his desk, asked Will to sit down. She took the armchair.

Dr. Melford brought his chair out from behind his desk and placed it catty-corner and rather close to Will's armchair. He sat down but did not speak immediately; he continued glancing through the top pages of a yellow legal pad. He had black hair, a high forehead, and a somewhat pug nose. His face was fairly round, and his chin, which was divided by a deep cleft, seemed to turn up at the tip. He looked, Will thought, rather like a bulldog; not a mature animal, but a puppy. Will wondered if this kind-looking man could help her.

Dr. Melford then explained the results of her tests. Psychological testing, he explained, was a little like charting a horoscope: It told one what to look out for, but not how. His chuckles attenuated when he saw Will was not amused. He could definitely tell her that she was not psychotic, nor apt to succumb to any type of serious mental illness. The sound of the doctor's voice was very like the feeling of Will's armchair—soft, comforting, enveloping—its tone could only be called therapeutic. An occupational hazard, she thought. For the rest, the doctor continued, he would use it as background material. He suggested they begin to talk; she knew an infinitely greater amount about herself than any test could tell him.

"It's strange being here," Will said.

"How so?" asked Dr. Melford.

"It's one of those situations everyone thinks about, like the doctor telling you you have a terminal disease, or the telephone call informing you that your husband has been in an accident. When it happens, it doesn't seem real."

"I wish you had better feelings about psychiatrists."

"I'm sorry, really—don't take offense." She paused. "I think I'm going to be a good patient, I'm already babbling my head off." Will looked up at the doctor and smiled.

The doctor then asked Will to tell him once again and in detail—the first time she had merely outlined the events—what had happened to her in the car and her kitchen. He wanted to know particularly her attitude toward the surrounding circumstances of those two days. Will answered as fully as she was able.

"Tell me," Dr. Melford said, "have you been depressed lately? Have you gone through a period of depression anytime within the last year?"

"I get down sometimes. No more than anyone else, though."

"Let's make a distinction, then. Have you felt 'down' for as long as one or two weeks, and have these periods been accompanied by listlessness? You might even have felt vaguely ill without knowing why."

"No, not really, Doctor."

"Call me Ray. Please." Their eyes met briefly, and then Dr. Melford looked away again. Will felt that he was shy and at the same time terrifically curious. His profession, Will thought, put him in the position of a child searching through his mother's dresser drawers, afraid of what he will find but too fascinated to stop. Will wanted to help him, to place a jewel box in the top left-hand drawer.

In desperation, she said, "There was one other crisis. The earthquake. But we all went through that."

"Tell me what it was like for you," Dr. Melford said neutrally.

"We live out in the north part of the valley, so we were fairly close to the epicenter. The wall in the living room cracked badly. We'll have to rebuild it."

"Describe that day for me."

"I woke up just before it started. Everyone says they did now, but I really did. Not because I sensed it was coming, but for the very good reason that Karen, our four-year-old, gets up about six-thirty every morning, and I could hear her playing in her room. I lay in bed, hoping to doze a while longer, when the quake started. Our bed rocked and yawed. I wasn't afraid—we have these things all the time, don't we?—but I wanted to make sure Karen was all right. She has a wall shelf in her room, filled with toys, and I was afraid it might fall on her. I got up and walked to her room.

"I was in the hall when the real shaking hit, when you knew it wasn't an ordinary earthquake. I had slipped into low-heeled pumps—when I was growing up, they told us to always have our shoes on in an emergency— but I hadn't really gotten them on properly. So in the hall I was still working my feet into them as I walked along, and then the shaking really hit and I fell. I hurt my ankle, and I had to crawl the rest of the way into Karen's room. Most of the toys did fall, but not the shelf itself. It wouldn't have mattered, anyway. When I reached her room, Karen was sitting on her desk on the opposite side of the room, watching the earthquake throw things around. She was delighted. Kids."

"Were you hurt badly?"

"No, my ankle was sore, but I carried Karen back into our bedroom after the shaking stopped. I guess I crawled into her room because I was afraid I would be knocked down again." She paused, then said in a voice filled with the surprise and merriment of revelation, "This might be it."

"Your feelings that week, tell me about them," Dr. Melford said quickly, eagerly.

"We had to move out. We were close to the dam that almost went, so we stayed with friends. This *is* strange."

"What?"

"I'd forgotten. I couldn't do anything that week. The friends we stayed with, the woman, Chris, she wouldn't let me help around the house. And then the church, where I work, was closed for a few days until it was inspected, and even when it was reopened no one could do anything—everyone was either evacuated or housing people who were. I *was* depressed. That's what's strange—I had forgotten. I was so depressed that I stopped doing the little things around Chris's house that she let me do. I lay on the couch all day and watched soap operas. I hate soap operas; I hated them while I was watching them. It's the most neurotic thing I've ever done."

"Maybe your pride simply wouldn't let you admit that you needed to escape in that way just then. Anything else about that period? What particularly impressed you about the earthquake?"

"What confuses me is that I wasn't frightened by it. If the trouble with my legs stems from the earthquake, wouldn't I have been tremendously frightened by the whole thing?"

"We don't always allow ourselves to feel what we should be feeling."

"Repression."

Dr. Melford waved his hand to the side and tilted his head, granting the appropriateness of the word and at the same time indicating that he found the use of jargon between them unnecessary.

"The one thing I do remember from that time," Will said, "is that one newscast reported the mountains had moved. Not noticeably, of course, but the San Gabriel range did shift. When I heard about it, I thought of a psalm my father used to read to us before our family went on a trip. Psalm 46: 'God is our refuge and strength, a very present help in trouble. Therefore will not we fear, though the earth be removed, and though the mountains be carried into the midst of the sea.' Farther on it says, 'The heathen raged, the kingdoms were moved: he uttered his voice, the earth melted.' I kept repeating those verses to myself. On the couch, right through the soap operas. I don't know why."

"Consolation?"

"It had that effect on my father."

They were silent for a time. Then Will said, "It's queer the way one feels one has 'permission' to recall these things because you're here. I'm also astounded that I could hide something like this from myself.

"But is this really going to work?" Will asked. "I mean, now that I know about being, shall we say, 'traumatized' by the earthquake, will the trouble with my legs really go away? I've always doubted—what can one call it?—the 'recognition theory.' "

"Do you want me to tell you that you're cured?"

"I wouldn't mind."

"We still have a lot to talk about. Next week. Make an appointment with my receptionist, Patty."

Will rose to go and extended her hand to Dr. Melford. "Thank-you, Ray," she said. "You've been a revelation." She turned and walked out the door, striding crisply. After shutting the inner office door behind her, she turned to see the receptionist, Patty, looking at her expectantly. Will nodded, swallowed the inarticulate sounds that failed to issue into speech, and walked out the outer office door.

In his office, Dr. Melford sat behind his desk and stared at his yellow legal pad. He wrote: "First Session." He waited a long time before he added: "Hysterical reaction? Existential crisis? What?"

Daniel Sunday parked his car in the driveway of his ranch-style home and went inside. He found Tricia, the teenage girl who babysat for them, in the living room doing her homework. His daughter, Karen, was there too, watching public television. She did not scream "Daddy!" and run and hug his legs, but looked around at him suspiciously. "Hello, Pigeon," he said, "good program?" By his manner she knew that he was not going to turn off the set. Contented, she turned back to the screen.

He paid Tricia before she left and sat down on the couch with the paper, waiting for the TV program to end, for the numbers one through ten to be shouted out for the last time that day. He wondered where his wife was and remembered that she had said she had a doctor's appointment. He did not know which doctor, or how late she would be. When she had told him about it, he had thought at first that the appointment concerned the trouble she was having with her legs. But when she had said doctor, she had turned down her lip, making such a distasteful expression that he concluded she meant gynecologist. He was to cook that night anyway, so she need not be home for another hour yet.

The television program ended, and he asked Karen if she would like to help him make dinner. She acquiesced. Work—tasks—provided the ground of their relationship. With his wife, Karen was what he thought of as a normal little girl; dependent, whimsical, hypersensitive, quintessentially childish. With him, Karen was all business.

In the kitchen he sat her in her old high chair, flipped the tray down over her head, and gave her a quarter of one of the potatoes he would boil that night and a dull vegetable peeler. Her legs dangled down far enough for her to rest her feet on one of the chair's crossbars. Her legs had just begun to grow again, and had become more fragile, fawnlike. Her golden, dutch-boy-cut hair fell about her cheeks as she worked tenaciously at her task.

She exuded an air of solemnity that was anachronistic rather than merely precocious; she might have been ninety-two-years old. Sometimes he called her "little Miss Humbug." Even though he accepted their relationship, he knew that her way with him kept him manageable, fended him off. He wondered if he appeared in her nightmares as the primal ogre. He wished that he had taken a larger role in caring for her basic needs—food and clean diapers—when she was an infant. The experts said now that performing these duties brought the father closer to the child.

He put a pot of water on for the potatoes and made a vinaigrette salad. He allowed Karen to cut up a few mushrooms while he watched and prayed that she would not somehow hurt herself with the dull knife. Then he took out the sole he had bought and prepared to dredge it in flour, so that he could cook it *meunière* style.

After all the preparations had been made for cooking and the fillets were lying on the sideboard in their white gloves of flour, Daniel poured himself a glass of V-8 juice and waited for his wife to arrive. He delivered the brutalized potato out of Karen's hands, gave her a carrot stick to eat, and told her to play in her room.

Alone in the kitchen, he relaxed. Cooking so preoccupied his attention that he forgot about the office and the stock market. At that moment, a taste of time was granted to him; he realized that he had come a long way in the transition from idolized youngest son to husband and father. Will had at first been his loyal supporter, working to put him through the Wharton School of Finance. And his career afterward had been and was a success. But then they had become so involved in the church that his work had become inessential to his real life—his life at the church. Will had taken the position of authority there. Now he was a man who took pleasure in cooking and providing for his family and believing in his wife's work. The taste of this was, surprisingly, sweet—the taste of freedom.

Daniel heard his wife's car in the driveway. She came in and announced her presence with a clearly projected "Hel-lo-o." Karen screamed and ran to her mother.

Daniel called out that he was in the kitchen.

Will came into the kitchen without Karen. She kissed Daniel in greeting—a long, rather exaggeratedly romantic kiss—and then rested her head on his chest for a moment. Taking both of his hands in hers, she pulled away from him, so that their arms formed a suspension bridge. Daniel saw then that the trip to the doctor had transformed his wife. Since the car incident, her face had had a drawn, ascetic cast to it; but now, her nicely full lips smiling broadly, the smile lines about her eyes the rays of two stars, she looked vital once more.

"I'm all right. I'm all right," Will said. She embraced him once more, kissed him repeatedly on his neck, cheeks, and lips. "I'm all right."

Daniel asked her to explain, and she did. At the conclusion of her speech, she pulled up her knee-length skirt, so that Daniel could see the heavier mesh of the top of her panty hose, and performed a few tap-dance steps. Daniel frowned.

"What'sa mattah, bustah? Don't these steppahs appeal to yah?" Will asked. "Don't these beautiful, perfectly healthy and soon to be psychologically fit legs appeal to you?"

"It's that easy?"

"What do you mean?"

"Did the doctor say *why* the earthquake had this effect on you?"

"He wanted to see me again," Will said. "But I don't think that's necessary now. You've got to understand, when I realized what had happened, I felt so great, I still feel great. I'm pretty sure I'm going to be okay. Aren't you glad?"

"Of course I am. I'm really, really glad."

"I don't believe you. I don't believe you for a minute," she said in a teasing voice. She came up to him and tickled him about the ribs (a particularly vulnerable area), her hands working over him like febrile ants. He reached out to hold her and thus crush her attack, but she went spinning away.

She continued spinning around the kitchen like a Turkish dancer, her arms two planing wings. She started singing, "The Sound of Music," in a loud, showboat voice. Daniel watched her apprehensively; he had seen her become hysterical in the past, laughing until she could only cry away her emotion. She passed close to the sink, and one flying arm knocked his V-8 juice glass into the sink, where it shattered. She stopped then, tried to get her breath and balance. Simultaneously, they saw Karen standing by the door.

Will tucked her chin in, contrite. "Can you handle this?" she asked, meaning, he supposed, the clean-up job and dinner. He nodded yes.

"Let's go into the living room and talk while Daddy gets dinner. Okay?" Will walked out with Karen through the swinging kitchen door.

Two days later, Will dreamed the first of what proved to be a series of nightmares. Upon awaking in the middle of the night, she could not recall what the dreams had been about. She did recall these nightmares later in the day, usually while she was going about a commonplace task. These recollections had the sudden vivacity of hallucinations, and so intervened between her and the daily world that she felt as locked inside the remembrance as she had been in the original dream.

In one dream, she attempted, Samsonlike, to hold up one of the bedroom walls against an earthquake, while her husband looked on and laughed. In another, she was swimming toward a distant shore when she realized that Daniel could not swim. She dove under the water to help him and then started to drown herself. These dreams came only once, but another dream recurred. In it she stood outside of herself and watched a figure whom she knew to be herself fall to the floor and then slowly dissolve into a malignant, white mass.

Although she did not immediately remember these nightmares, she awoke from them experiencing the most palpable sense of dread. The taste of iron was in her mouth and her skin prickled. Worst of all, she did not feel free of the dream; she felt trapped, as if constrained in a chair, enclosed within an airtight glass booth. To escape the dread, she often got out of bed and went into the living room to pace. There she reminded herself of who she was and of all she had to be thankful for. Eventually, when she had learned that she would not be able to sleep until almost dawn, she used the time to read the Bible and pray. She had never prayed as she did during these vigils: The intensity with which she petitioned God frightened her at times.

Over a period of several weeks the dread grew so strong in the night that it invaded Will's days. Dread kept her from accomplishing her tasks. The first time she called to cancel a church appointment, embarrassment held her at the phone for fifteen minutes while she debated whether to dial. But phone call followed phone call, and soon she was adept at making excuses, though each excuse inflicted another wound to her self-respect. More and more she sat idle in the armchair in the living room, looking out through the sliding glass doors to the backyard. Dread brought a strange silence to the world, muffling it. She felt herself withdrawing, pulling back, trying to feel secure within the fortress of herself. She knew all the time, however, that in seeking security, she found only a cool oblivion, the dread's silence.

At times, her soul rebelled. She chanted the phrase, *I've got to get hold of myself,* as if it were a spell which would summon her latent resources of power. She reminded herself of the struggles she had been through—with her father when her mother died, with Daniel when he was in business school. But nothing alleviated her profound sense of impotence.

More and more she left her armchair and went to her bed, until she was sleeping up to eighteen hours a day. She complained to Daniel of amorphous physical disorders: She was tired, her bones ached, she felt feverish. He suggested that she return to the doctor. Will knew that their family physician would send her back to the psychiatrist, Dr. Melford. She stopped complaining. She then tried to make Daniel believe that she was all right by showing more energy around the house when he came home. But she knew Daniel was not fooled. She needed the masquerade, however; it kept her from acting on what she knew to be the truth—that she was suffering from severe depression.

About a month after she had become depressed, still several weeks before Easter, Will decided to call her father. Dr. White and Will were very close; they corresponded once a week, long letters given to literary fancies. But Will had not written in the last two weeks; she did not want to tell him about her depression, but she did not want to lie, either. Instead, during this time, she used the image of her father—who he was, what he stood for—as her debating partner, turning her private soliloquies concerning her problem into imaginary colloquies: She asked the questions, he gave the putative answers. This game proved safe but unsatisfactory, a placebo without real analgesic power. Finally, she needed to hear his voice.

Her father was to Will nothing if not the voice of authority. He taught apologetics and homiletics at a seminary in Louisville, Kentucky. He was the latest of the many Whites who had given their lives to the Christian ministry. Her father's voice, besides possessing the authority of a father and scholar, resonated with history. Growing up conscious of being a White, Will never had many doubts about her faith. But now that that faith was being tested, she hesitated to rely on the person who had given her that faith; for if he failed her, she would be adrift, indeed. Still, sitting in the kitchen at the breakfast table, she dialed.

His voice came on the line: It sounded distant, somehow filtered by so much space, and yet at the same time immediate and clear. His greetings had a gruff edge; his voice needed to unlimber before it became a melodic, oratorical instrument.

"Papa," Will said, "I wanted to talk with you."

"I presumed that's why you called," Dr. White said.

"I mean, I need to talk with you."

"You're not having more trouble with your legs?"

"No, but yes . . . in a way. I'm depressed, Papa. I've never been so depressed in my life. It's horrible. You can't believe it."

"Angel, it's natural to be upset after an illness."

"Papa, the depression *is* the illness, its new form. I went to a psychiatrist. He said I might get depressed."

"I've never had any truck with those fellows, myself. You really went to one?"

"Yes. I felt the same way you do, but he actually helped me. I thought he had cured me."

"What was he like?"

"A fairly young man. He asked a lot of questions. But the point is that he connected the trouble I'm having with the big earthquake. It knocked me down, did you know that?"

"You've lost me, Angel."

"The earthquake, Papa. It must have really frightened me, and I'm having a delayed reaction to it."

"But nothing substantial happened to the house, did it?"

"The *house* isn't having the reaction. I am!"

"All right now, calm down. How can I help you?"

"While we were evacuated, staying with our friends, I kept repeating the forty-sixth psalm to myself. The one we used to read before we went on vacations. Did you know that until I was twenty-one, I never went on any trip without reciting that psalm?"

"It's one of the loveliest poems ever written," Dr. White said.

"But why did we read it?" Will asked.

"As an invocation of God's protective power."

"When does an invocation become an incantation?"

"I see what you're saying, but I disagree. I never believed for a moment that prayer is magic."

"I think I have a superstitious bent, then."

"Your faith, Wilfred, has always been the most beautifully natural thing. Don't talk like that."

"Well, the psalm itself has begun to bother me, too. In the first few verses it seems that God stands behind events. I don't like that idea; it seems irresponsible of Him."

"Angel, remember Job? Remember what the Lord says to Job out of the tempest? He doesn't really answer Job's questions. In fact, he mainly talks a lot about having made the crocodile."

"The point, though, is that we can't always understand why God does things, but God's design is there nevertheless. And God has promised to deliver the believer in times of trouble. You need to claim God's promise. Remember Daniel in the lion's den, how the ravens brought food to Elijah, how Peter was set free from prison by the earthquake. Pray and wait on the Lord. He will deliver you. I know He will."

"Papa, I have prayed. I've spent I don't know how many nights pacing the living-room floor, unable to sleep . . . ." Her voice broke. She felt the same humiliation she had always felt when, as a little girl, she had broken down in front of her father.

"Think about the old lady," Dr. White said, "who petitioned the judge in the Bible. She bothered him, pestered him, wouldn't relent until he gave her justice. You've got to have the same pertinacity. It's hard, I know."

"It's hell, that's what it is. I really don't think I'm going to make it."

"Wilfred—look, Wilfred—remember what the last part of the psalm says, 'Be still, and know that I am God.' You're all right, you've got a good husband, a lovely child; nothing is really wrong. You've just got to be still and wait this thing out. It will pass. We don't stay frightened forever."

"I don't know, Papa. Maybe I should go back to the psychiatrist. I know you're telling me the truth. I've thought about what you've said, but throwing Bible verses at my problems just doesn't seem to help. Maybe I've really got a deep psychological flaw."

"If you go back to that man, Wilfred, he'll put you on drugs. Do you want Karen to have an addict for a mother?"

"Don't be reactionary, Papa, it doesn't become you."

"I'm sorry. I just don't like those fellows; half of them are more sick than their patients."

"And no one in our family has ever gone to one."

"Well, we haven't."

"Well, I have."

"Do what *you* think is best, then."

"Oh no, I won't let you be mad. I'm sick. It's an implicit rule that the parent is not allowed to get mad at the child when she is sick."

"I'm not mad, Angel. I do wish you wouldn't keep saying you're sick, though. 'Mental illness' has always seemed to me an abominable expression."

"Upset, then."

"Good. Why don't you call me in a few days, collect? Please."

"I will. Thanks Papa. You know I love you."

"You'll be fine, Angel. You'll be fine."

"Good-bye then."

"Yes, good-bye."

Will knew that her father was right: Her deliverance lay in the Lord's hands. But if the Lord used doctors to heal the physically afflicted, she reasoned, He shouldn't be prejudiced against using psychiatrists in cases like her own.

Twice a week for the several weeks remaining until Easter, Will sat in the big armchair in Dr. Melford's office, avoiding the doctor's eyes by scanning the titles on his bookshelves and talking with him. There were no revelations, as there had been on her first visit.

The doctor's and Will's discussions resolved into one circular argument. Will described her symptoms and complained that it was becoming increasingly difficult for her to handle her daily life. The doctor suggested, subtly at first and then with greater force, that her symptoms expressed a subliminal desire to be dependent. He urged her to give in to her desire to be weak, to learn to be comfortable with this desire. A wrestler, he said, can sometimes extricate himself from a difficult hold by suddenly giving way to the pressure from his opponent.

He was asking the impossible, Will explained. She had been taught to be in control of herself. A short homily on original sin and the need to be vigilant against man's lower nature usually followed. Dr. Melford would then blow out his cheeks and put his hand to his mouth.

At the end of their second session, Dr. Melford wrote out two prescriptions. One was for a tranquilizer, Librium, and the other was for a mood elevator, Tofranil, to combat her depression. Will thought of what her father had said and was wryly amused that his scenario—she was not going to be an addict, after all—had partially come to pass. She filled the prescriptions but did not take the pills regularly, until the doctor explained that unless she followed his dosage instructions, the pills would be ineffective.

To Will's surprise, the pills helped. She found the relationship of chemistry to psychic well-being disturbing; that the insubstantial, her mental state, could be controlled by a substance, the pills, violated her sense of the divorce between the physical and the spiritual. She was, however, grateful that the pills allowed her to resume an almost normal schedule.

By the beginning of Easter week, Will's condition had greatly improved. She was sleeping normally and working a long day. Under the doctor's guidance, she had cut back on her medication. She had always thought "being happy" a poor ideal, and yet now that she had experienced weeks of intense unhappiness, she had changed her mind.

Yet part of her longed for her depression to return. With and without her psychiatrist, she had spent time thinking about her depression; she had written at length to her father about it; her meditations had created an enormous appetite to know why the earthquake had affected her as it had. She felt that as the symptoms departed, she was losing touch with the secret. She decided that on Monday of Easter week she would lock herself into the guest room of her home, and there, like Jacob wrestling with the angel, she would fast and pray until the Lord spoke the word she needed to hear.

That morning she explained to Daniel what she intended to do. He did not ask any questions—which was a sign that he had serious doubts about the wisdom of what she proposed. He promised to take Karen to nursery school and pick her up and manage their meals for as long as Will stayed in the guest room. After her husband and daughter left the house, Will went to the freezer and took out a loaf of French bread. She filled a lucite pitcher with water and placed it on a tray next to the bread and, carrying her provisions before her, she went into the guest room.

The guest room had only one window, which faced due north. Consequently, it was a rather dark room and had been painted a bright yellow to compensate for this. The room was also rather small; the two single beds there left just enough space for one to maneuver comfortably around them. In the corner by the window sat a small desk. Will put the tray down on the desk and took out the Bible she kept in the middle drawer.

Through the rest of the morning, she read the Psalms. At first, she only planned to read the forty-sixth and twenty-third and perhaps a few others, but she found the themes of the psalms—repentance, deliverance, praise—exactly suited to her meditational needs. With the psalmist, she cried out against her metaphorical enemies, the causes of her depression; she called on the Lord, asking how long it would be before He delivered her; and then she assured herself of His deliverance by contemplating the character of God, His righteousness,

His justice, His power, His love.

About noon she ate a quarter of the loaf of bread and drank a glass of water. In the afternoon, she began to pray. She took a pillow from one of the beds and knelt on it beside the desk, her makeshift *prie-dieu*. She prayed with the intention of emptying her mind, of expressing every emotion, every impulse of the will, down to the velleities. She found that, primed by sufficient time, her thoughts poured forth; they began to carry her along, unexpected sluices quickened the already frightening pace, eddies added spin. The intensity with which she prayed seemed neurotic to her; she wondered if she should have taken her medication that morning. But then, she thought, any true confrontation with the holy would be frightening: Fear gave birth to hope.

By the time she finished praying, it was night. Her mind was calm. She watched the moon rise and the stars come out, and she waited. She waited and watched all through the night; her mind did not wander, nor did it attend to any particular thought or set of images; it had found a profound and sublime silence.

In the morning she stood up. Her knees were sore, her limbs stiff. Yet she did not feel the disorientation of having missed a night's sleep; perhaps she *had* slept; she could not tell. She only knew that it was right to get up now and go fix breakfast. The Lord had spoken. She did not know exactly when, but she knew that sometime during the night the words "Trust Me" had come to her, and these words were accompanied by the conviction that this message was all she needed to hear. She was absolutely certain that from now on she was going to be all right. And so, before she fixed breakfast, she went into the bathroom and flushed her pills down the toilet.

On Wednesday morning of Easter week, Will attended the staff meeting at the church. Afterward, Reverend March, the pastor of the church, asked Will to accompany him to his office. There was a matter he wanted to speak with her about.

Reverend March's office was probably the most unusual room in the church. There were no windows; bookshelves covered most of three walls, from the floor to the ceiling. The remaining area was panelled with wood which had been decoratively hand carved; a scrollwork pediment ostentatiously topped the door. The room contained three desks, two of which were at the foot of the room, piled with books and papers. On the wall behind the main desk, a row of framed photographic portraits of the former pastors of the church was to be found. In the middle of the room, standing alone like a small tree, was a four-sided bookcase that rotated; in this bookcase Reverend March kept his dictionaries and frequently used reference books. The room had that certain atmosphere of mustiness and arranged clutter common to old mens'-club libraries.

Will sat down in a spindle-backed chair and Reverend March sat on the side of his desk, one foot on the ground and one in the air. The pastor was long limbed, with bold features; bent into his nonchalant posture against the desk, his body looked like a discombobulated spring mechanism that would not quite set into place. Beads of perspiration broke out along the imaginary hairline of his bald crown. He was reluctant to speak, he breathed heavily, he looked down at the toe of his airborne foot. Will guessed that the pastor wanted to talk about her health and the way she had been handling her job; the tension between them, she thought, would all disappear if she just knew how to tell him about her revelation. But strangely, before this man of God, the very word *revelation* embarrassed her.

"I've tried not to pry, Will," Reverend March said. "But we all know you haven't been feeling well. There comes a certain point when I, as your boss, have to know what I can expect from you. I'm sorry, I don't mean to sound so stuffy."

"Pastor, I understand. I didn't say anything, I guess, because I didn't know what to say. I've had an odd reaction to the earthquake. I've been to doctors about this, and we've pinned down the trouble. But it's over now, and I'm definitely going to be all right."

"When I said, 'there comes a point,' Will, I didn't mean now. The point passed a while ago. I talked to your husband about your problem. He explained. I also called your psychiatrist. He couldn't be specific, of course, but he was also helpful."

Will became extraordinarily angry; blood rushed to her cheeks, her heart pounded. Words failed her. They seemed too soft, malleable, rubbery; she wanted to hit back with iron.

"I've made a decision, Will. One that I think best for you and the church. I've decided to divide your responsibilities with Mrs. Jeffers. She will take charge of the nursery and kindergarten departments, you'll still have the primary and juniors."

"I cannot work with Mrs. Jeffers, Pastor."

"Speaking humanly, she is not my all-time favorite

person. She will, however, be a dedicated worker."

"I cannot work with that woman! She drives me crazy now!"

"I've already hired her, Will. Don't get your back up like this. You need time to recover, to recoup your mental energy. Try to see this as an unexpected portioning out of divine grace."

"Grace? Grace? Grace? This isn't grace, it's a conspiracy."

"I would have talked to you personally about it, but your husband thought it would upset you: If you tried to keep up appearances for the sake of holding on to the job, he thought you might break. I'm only talking to you now because we all see that you are feeling better."

Will began to cry uncontrollably, her face transformed into a mass of wet drapery.

"Will," Reverend March said in a dumbfounded voice, "I'm sorry, I truly am. Please stop. I don't understand this from you. Please, stop now."

Reverend March stepped to her and put his hands on her shoulders to comfort her. His touch revived Will's anger. She pushed him away from her with such unexpected force, that, except for the desk behind him, he might have fallen over. While Reverend March looked on in hurt, stupefied silence, Will took up her bag and hurriedly left the office.

On her way home Will drove quickly, starting and stopping abruptly, turning at such speed that she had to lean into the turns against the car's centrifugal force. She looked forward to being home with the expectations of someone who has been on a long, anxious journey; she wanted the reassurance of the familiar, to run her hand over her silklike bedspread. If she could only be at home for a while, she thought, the events troubling her might be seen objectively, as external forces that could be coped with from a secure center, the carapace of her home.

But midway there, she decided to head for Karen's nursery school. She would only truly be home when Karen was there with her. The child would help her recover the image of herself as a mature, responsible woman, someone whom others depended on.

Will did not go to the school's main office, as she knew she ought; she proceeded directly down the long hall to room N-4. She looked through the oblong door window before she entered. The children were arranged in three horseshoe clusters around diminutive tables. The teacher and her assistant bent way over from the waist, helping their pupils at their tasks. Gradually, more and more suspicious little faces turned to stare at Will. She entered the classroom then, walked straight over to Karen, and took the child into her arms before she had time to put down her crayon. Karen wrapped her legs around her mother's waist, leaned back, and gave Will a quizzical look. The teacher came over.

In a preemptory voice Will explained that she was going to take Karen home early. But then, unexpectedly, Karen demanded to be put down. Slightly embarrassed, Will complied with the child's request, and hand in hand they walked out of the classroom. All the way to the car Karen was silent and wore an expression of confused wariness; she kept stealing sideways looks at her mother. Will realized that she ought to explain the situation to Karen; but she was utterly unable to do so and said nothing. By the time they reached the car, the silence between them was haunting.

Will drove home in the same hurried manner. Halfway through the short trip, Karen began to play as if she too were driving the car. She drove with intensity; she peered ahead like a hunter stalking game, and her hands were balled up into white-knuckled fists. Seeing Karen, Will suddenly became conscious that she was gripping the steering wheel as if to strangle the life out of the car. She stopped for a light, dropped her hands, and took in several deep breaths. And then, in a determinedly light-hearted voice, she said, "Almost home, Karen. Almost home now."

At home, Will brought Karen into the living room and sat down beside her on the couch. Will proposed to have a chat with the child, to discuss nonconsequential subjects as one would before a dinner party. But Karen did not respond to Will's prompting questions. Her head lolled from side to side, and she whined.

Will decided to make tea with lunch, in order to put Karen into the appropriate mood. But when she had fixed cream-cheese-and-jelly sandwiches on raisin bread, prepared the tea, and served all of this to Karen, the child wandered around the living room, passing a sandwich from hand to hand and smearing the jelly that clung to her fingers on everything she touched. Will ordered Karen to sit down. She spoke sharply about Karen's lack of manners.

The child sat on the couch again, her eyes downcast, wearing a disconsolate expression. She slowly chewed the remainder of her sandwich. She was quite good, Will knew, at picking up on her parents' moods; she would not talk now because, through the most elemental of chemistries, she knew the confusion her mother was feeling, and she felt as trapped and smothered by that feeling as the childlike part of Will's personality did.

Will found that she had little appetite. The tea produced an uneasiness in her bowels. The jelly marks on the TV and the stereo cabinet and the walls made her aware of the state of her living room. Daniel had left one of his sweaters next to where she sat on the couch, piles of newspapers sat by the easy chairs whose cushions needed to be turned and fluffed, the bookshelves were crooked, and there was even a cobweb in the far corner next to the sliding glass doors. She realized these faults were minor, trifles, and yet they seemed to articulate the menacing disarrangement in her own life.

Then Karen put her head in Will's lap. The child allowed her mother to stroke her thick, short blond hair. The moment Will had been seeking seemed very near. If they could only be still together a little longer, that stillness would prove stronger than the world. But the child could not get comfortable; she began to squirm, to maneuver herself by grabbing at her mother, pinching handholds that were indeed painful. Will pulled Karen up by the hands and told her to go into her room to play.

Will stayed in the living room. She would not have been able to say why, but she had the definite feeling— perhaps it consisted of a tightness in her chest—that she had entered the zone in which her legs might give way. A moment or two later she felt dizzy, and she put her hands out to either side, like the ropes that steady tents.

She felt the first tremor. It started as a quivering in her legs; the amplitude of the vibration modulated into a long, steady sway that passed into her torso, shaking her violently. Nothing in the house moved, so she knew the tremor to be imaginary; that is, confined to the territory, the landscape, of her body. The second tremor broke within her much more quickly and was of shorter duration, although it registered with the same intensity on her private Richter scale. Tremor after tremor came. The edifice of herself was breaking apart; she would be reduced to stone, dust, and ashes if she did not escape somehow. Yet she was afraid to move, afraid to find herself helpless, an hysterical paraplegic once more. She ran to the bathroom, hoping that by running she would magically displace the weight that would cause her legs to give way.

In the bathroom she found that she had outdistanced the epicenter of the tremors. She did not, however, find what she knew would stop the entire experience: her pills. When she had thrown her pills away, she had, as always, been methodical and thorough. She *had* kept the bottles, so if she could manage to control her hands, she could call the drugstore and they would deliver a refill.

From the back of the house she heard a decisive crash, a plangent crescendo, a sound that cut time, interposing an unknown splice. Will, terrified, considered the possibility that perhaps there had been an earthquake after all. She waited. Instinct then gave her the strength to become once again the protective mother; she hurried back to Karen's room.

She found Karen sitting on her desk, her legs dangling back and forth, the wall-size toy shelf on the floor with various broken toys scattered around its edges. Will did not know how, but she knew Karen had done this. The

child's face had taken on the cool, amoral, slightly de-
fiant, interested expression it wore when she tested her
mother.

Will's hysteria resurrected. She screamed at the child,
"Get out of the house! You've ruined everything! You've
ruined my house! Get out! Now! Go!"

As Will approached Karen she could see the child's
face cloud, the wailing commence. Karen cried,
"Mommy, don't! Mommy!"

Will continued to scream for Karen to leave the house.
She took the child up, lifted her off the desk with her
hands about Karen's shoulders, set her on her feet, and
began pushing her out the bedroom door. At the
threshold she gave her a particularly urgent shove; the
child tripped over a toy wooden bus, and, propelled by
her mother's shove, she sailed for several feet before
hitting her head against the hall wall and falling to the
floor. Will's first thought was that she had killed her only
child. But then she heard Karen's wailing renew itself.

Will felt tremendously relieved that she could comfort
the child now and within an hour or two they might both
forget the incident. She picked the child up and tried to
hold her, but Karen backed away from her mother, down
the hall. Her face was contorted by paroxysms of howling wails—absolute, terrified protests against what had
occurred. Will did not understand; then she saw that
Karen was holding her right forearm with her left hand,
as if to support it. Karen's right hand was twisted in an
impossible fashion back toward the outside of her elbow.
Will took a step closer and she could see the bone, pink
with blood, at the wrist.

Will ran past Karen to the telephone, to call an

ambulance—she knew she could not drive in her present state. The white and orange van pulled up to their house without any siren fanfare. To and from the hospital Karen did not allow her mother to touch her. When they returned home, Karen of her own accord went to bed, sucking the thumb of the hand that was mostly encased in her new cast. Will retired to her room.

The house was quiet when Daniel arrived home that evening. He called out to his wife and child, but no one answered. His bedroom door was locked. He became apprehensive, but experienced his fear as embarrassment; he had come upon the strangely hallowed ground of an event, and he did not quite know what to do with himself.

Karen was still asleep when he entered her room. That she should be asleep in the midst of her chaotic, toy-strewn room sounded an eerie, melodramatic organ chord. While standing by her railed bed, he saw the cast, heavy, weaponlike, so foreign to the tender scene of his daughter sleeping. He roused Karen, sat her up in bed. She put her arms around his neck and tried to slip back into sleep. But his questions pricked her awake. He asked what had happened, had the shelf fallen on her? When she said, "Mommy. Mommy pushed me. Mommy was angry," Daniel was not sure that sleep had not refashioned the experience through its associative power.

Distantly but compellingly the three-tone doorbell rang. Two policemen were at the door. They were young, athletic, handsome; they looked more like col-

lege students circa 1960—the year Daniel graduated—
than marshals of the law. They asked uneasily if they
might come in.

The shorter of the two explained that they had to make
out a report for the Child Welfare Division concerning
the circumstances surrounding his daughter's unfortu-
nate accident. The policemen explained that his wife
had claimed responsibility for what had happened,
though from the hospital's preliminary report she could
not be blamed in any legal sense. Still, they had to know
exactly what had happened.

Just then Will entered the living room from the hall-
way. She wore a simple, deep purple dress with a loop of
pearls at the neck, a black hat with a veil, and black
low-heeled pumps. She carried her bag, the strap looped
over her forearm. She looked as if she were about to go
calling on an ancient aunt, or attend a funeral. She
clasped her hands feverishly, and her eyes were very
cold and blue.

"I've been waiting," she said, evidently to the policemen. "Handcuffs aren't necessary, but you follow regu-
lations. Don't bother with my rights."

"Lady," the shorter policeman said, "we haven't come
to arrest you. We just want to talk."

"You *must* arrest me. I explained at the hospital. I
abused my child."

"Even if you did, we wouldn't arrest you. Not the first
time."

Daniel signalled to the taller policeman, but the man
did not see him.

"You must arrest me! I'm guilty. Guilty . . . as sin, as

my father used to say." Will laughed—a wild, manic laugh.

"Fortunately for you, Lady, it's not up to you to say if you're guilty."

"It is up to me. I know what happened."

The taller policeman finally saw Daniel's signals. They adjourned to a corner of the room, where Daniel explained that Will had been under a psychiatrist's care. If they could just postpone their investigation until his wife became herself again? Daniel knew that he was handling the matter as if his wife were no longer responsible for her actions. She did not, however, seem truly crazy to him, only operating on the frontier of her own peculiar logic.

The two policemen conferred and soon thereafter made a tactical retreat. As soon as they left, Will walked stiffly back into her room.

Daniel telephoned Dr. Melford. He told the doctor's answering service about the emergency; his wife was undergoing a crisis, which, frankly, had him scared. The doctor returned his call within an hour. After Daniel explained to him what he knew and could surmise, the doctor asked Daniel if Will was taking her medication. Skirting a description of Will's "revelation"—it might sound crazier now than at another time—Daniel explained that Will had been feeling better and had thrown the pills away. Dr. Melford instructed Daniel to refill the prescriptions and see to it that Will took the proper dosages. Dr. Melford wanted to see Will in the morning, if that was at all possible. Daniel promised to follow the doctor's instructions, thanked him, and hung up.

That night and next day Will refused to come out of her room. Daniel stayed home from work. When he was not taking care of Karen, he spent a great deal of the day standing outside his bedroom door, mostly listening, but sometimes delivering monologues to Will, encouraging her to come out, to take her medicine, to give him a sign that she was all right.

Occasionally, he heard her move about the room, so he knew she had not physically harmed herself; otherwise, he would have called the rescue squad or whomever one called and had them take her out of there. He considered having her taken out, anyway. He wondered if he should call Dr. Melford and ask whether she should be hospitalized. He refrained, though—he could not quite convince himself that she did not have the right to wait out the agony of what she had done in the solitude of her room; he wanted to protect his wife's emotions from being labelled "sick" by outsiders.

He also called Reverend March to ask his advice and learned of Will's demotion and how she had received the news hours before the accident. Daniel had discussed Will's psychic well-being with Reverend March because he had wanted the pastor to understand why Will might not seem up to par. He had not thought that the pastor would use the information against her, though he realized Reverend March believed he was doing Will a kindness by reducing her responsibilities—they did not need the money, after all. Still, Daniel felt guilty for having betrayed his wife, and thus felt responsible for what she was going through now. He even felt himself to be an accomplice in her abuse of Karen. He wanted only to help, and yet he could not act; the contradictions in the situation rendered his will a useless instrument.

On Friday, Daniel decided to take a risk and leave the

house. His constant surveillance might turn Will's retreat into a test of wills, might pressure her to continue
what she might want to end. If he demonstrated faith in
her recovery, she might accept it herself. So he took
Karen to nursery school and went to the office for the
morning, planning to return with his daughter at noon.

When Will heard Daniel and Karen leave the house,
she felt as if she had been liberated from a confining
instrument of torture. She had been in retreat from them
and yet, through the two nights and a day, she had felt
them about her, their breath, their wet skin. She had
only been able to avoid detection by moving quickly
from place to place or by keeping very still in one protective corner.

She opened her bedroom door and walked down the
hall. By Karen's bedroom door, she heard a scream
which perfectly mimicked Karen's voice stretched to
horrific limits. Will stopped and stood still with her eyes
closed. She wanted to look down, but she did not, because she knew that she would see Karen lying before
her. She pivoted around and trotted back to her bathroom.

Will sat on the tiled floor by the tub. Her hands balled
up into fists, her stomach muscles tightened, her jaw
clenched, and her lips pursed so that they turned almost
white: out of frustration, she was trying to fight off the
madness through sheer bodily control. For she knew that
she was, indeed, fighting madness; while the circumfer-
ence of her mind went through the experience, there
remained a calm center which told her that her fears and

this voice were unreasonable, imaginary. The calm center also told her to relax, to go to the medicine cabinet and take the pills which Daniel had ordered: the pills which would make the voice go away—the pills which would allow her to sleep for the first time in three days.

She found the child-proof bottle containing fifty Librium tranquilizers on the middle shelf. She filled a glass of water and took two tablets. Given her state of mind, she doubted that would be enough, so she took two more. After that, she did not think about what she was doing. She simply swallowed the tablets—up to ten at a time—until the bottle was empty.

Will sat back down on the edge of the tub and thought about suicide; she had never thought about it before, but now that she was committing the act, it seemed a very good idea. She refused to live in a world in which inexplicable and uncontrollable disasters like earthquakes occurred. She refused to live in a world in which unwittingly people hurt other people, as she had injured her daughter. Most of all, she refused to live in a world in which unreal voices and images appeared; a world in which she could not even control her own mind.

The pills affected her quickly. All of the nerve endings throughout her body seemed to uncurl like so many blossoms, to luxuriate in the ultraviolet warmth of the chemical sun. And then the drug seemed not a sun but a warm, pacific sea, and she a migratory creature swimming farther and farther out toward another instinctual shore.

She walked from her bathroom back into her bedroom and lay down on the bed. If Karen found her there, she would presume that Mommy was sleeping. On the bed she began to lose consciousness of herself as a singular being; she felt her body at once expand and dematerialize. Soon there was only a lone, persistent signal, the pulsation of her thoughts, that she could recognize as herself.

At the last she wondered if the Roman Catholics were right in believing that God damned suicides. But then her father's belief in "once saved, always saved" came back to her; it did not reassure her, it delighted her—she experienced a black joy—a giddy, spiraling sensation. In losing her life, she would gain a victory over God that she had been obscurely seeking for a long time now: She would force Him to receive her autonomous soul into His kingdom. With an extreme effort of will, she regained awareness of her hand; she clenched it and immediately lost consciousness.

Daniel discovered Will when he returned home shortly before noon. The psychotropic drug she had taken did not have the toxic power, the mortal kick, of a barbiturate. Its milder action allowed the doctors to save Will's life. Daniel was at her bedside when she awoke on Sunday in the psychiatric ward of the local Presbyterian hospital.

When she awoke she was—in a frighteningly literal fulfillment of a metaphor—newborn. Daniel saw her eyes open; the blindness of sleep left them, they focused for an instant, and then took on the subaqueous look of an infant.

After three days, Will was transferred to a private

mental hospital. During this time and for the next two weeks Will would not or could not form words. She expressed herself in breathy nonsense syllables, urgent whines when she wanted something, placated cooing when she was content. She refused hard food and had to be bottle-fed by a nurse. She would not walk, though she took pleasure in crawling about her room. Daniel watched over her while she was at play, crawling among the toys the children's ward had sent over. The incongruity of the situation angered him: he wanted to slap Will and tell her that her act wasn't funny. Then he realized that would be "treating her like a child," and he experienced a depth of sadness he had never known before.

Slowly, Will's behavior matured. She did not walk, but she did sit up in a wheelchair and allow herself to be carted around the hospital. She began to talk in short, declarative sentences, and she spent much of her time singing Sunday-school choruses to herself. She soon reached a plateau, however, beyond which she did not seem willing to venture. The doctors estimated her age at four. She began to treat Daniel as if he were her father, calling him "Daddy," and asking his permission to watch television or play with her toys. It became clear to everyone that Will was assuming the place of her own child, Karen.

Dr. Melford came to Daniel and told him that he thought Will's father should come visit his daughter, if they could possibly afford the expense. Daniel surmised that the doctor hoped to shock Will out of her present role. He found the doctor's strategy primitive in the most pejorative sense and told him so. The doctor argued that though Will's resort to symbolic behavior was dramatic, he did not believe the logic of the symbolism had much of a hold on her mind. He believed that she would quit the role anyway, given sufficient time, but he wanted to start the healing process as soon as possible. He *was* worried about her not being able to walk as yet.

Daniel picked Dr. White up at the Los Angeles International Airport. Dr. White was a tall, big-boned man with an open face and rather small, almost feminine features. His hair was still thick, though white. He looked young and handsome enough to brag, without a scintilla of regret, that he was a grandfather.

Daniel and his father-in-law approved of each other. Their relationship was grounded in two facts: Dr. White had raised a lovely woman, and Daniel provided that woman with a suitable home. Daniel had, nonetheless, committed the aboriginal crime of taking Will from her father. Though they were civilized, in ays sophisticated, the crime was no less a crime, the wound under the bandage no less disturbing. And so their relationship always had the character of two enemies, tribes, nations who have fought, resolved their differences, and never quite forgotten. Will's hospitalization reawakened the memory, gave a contentious edge to their preliminary talk about Will. They were two much-better-than-average men, and yet this grievance was between them, and driving along on the way to the hospital, Daniel felt it.

When Daniel, Dr. White, and Dr. Melford came into Will's room, she was sitting on her bed, dressed in the light blue boy's pajamas which Daniel had bought for her one Christmas at her request. She played with a doll between her crossed legs. Her short hair was mussed and dirty, her face lean, her skin dry. Most of the time she had the sober, resolved appearance of hospital patients. But when she smiled at the doll—when her parody of childishness masked her suffering in such a way that the mask was not a mask, but rather the very face of that suffering—then she looked mad. Daniel had grown used to seeing Will this way, but now he saw her through Dr. White's naive eyes and was afraid.

Dr. White approached Will's bed, reached out, and took her hand. Will looked up at him. She leaned away, letting her arm go limp; she did not draw her hand away from his, but she disclaimed participation in this small gesture of affectionate possession.

"Hello, Angel," Dr. White said. "How are you feeling?"

Will took her hand away. She turned to Daniel. "Who is this man, Daddy?" she asked.

"It's your father."

Will considered this proposition for a moment. Dr. Melford had told Daniel that Will's trust in him must not be jeopardized. If she could not reconcile Daniel's and Dr. White's presence, then Dr. White was to leave immediately. Daniel had not expected the crisis to be reached so quickly. But Will's expression became so delicate and pure—he had never seen anything like it before—that he knew she was deciding now.

"No, he's not," Will said. Even though she denied her father, Daniel was not disappointed, for the childish mask had slipped: She spoke as an adult.

"Why not?" Daniel asked.

Will turned her face to the side. "He's not," she said.

"Why not?" Dr. Melford asked.

"He doesn't know," she said.

"What, Angel? What don't I know?" Dr. White asked.

"You don't know," she said vehemently. She was becoming anxious. Daniel thought they had better break off and try again the next day.

"I know you," Dr. White said. "I know you're my little girl, Wilfred."

"No! You don't know!"

"Maybe we'd better let Will rest now," Daniel said. He was surprised when his father-in-law obeyed, turned, and walked out the door.

Outside in the hall Daniel wanted to tell Dr. White how beneficial he thought his visit had been, but the older man, having lost his composure, kept walking and disappeared into a men's room.

Dr. Melford then came out of Will's room and he and Daniel conferred. Daniel said that he believed his father-in-law's visit had caused a certain separation between Will and her role. Dr. Melford hesitated, seemed slightly averse to assenting quickly to a layman's opinion, but then agreed. Daniel suggested that they think about having Karen come in. The doctor absolutely forbade this, warning Daniel against allowing his hopes for a quick cure to lead him into irresponsible actions.

Nevertheless, two nights later Daniel brought Dr. White and Karen to see Will. He worried whether Karen would be allowed to see her mother. Children visited patients in the ward where Will's room was located, but usually they had to be screened first by the head nurse. The night nurses knew little about the exact nature of the cases, however, and Daniel hoped that Dr. Melford had put nothing down on Will's chart to indicate that Karen should not be allowed in. As it happened, the nurse passed them through without looking at the records.

Daniel also worried about the effect the visit would have on Karen. He knew that the world chiefly appeared to his daughter as chaotic, unmanageable, and that her parents' ability to manage, to cope, was the basis of her faith that the chaos could be kept at arms' length. If she understood that her mother had succumbed to the world's intractableness, had forsaken her position as forward scout of the world's pathways and retreated back into childhood, how might Karen respond?

Still, other factors convinced Daniel that the experiment should be tried. Karen had seen her mother taken off to the hospital. Children were not supposed to be aware of death, but Karen acted as if her mother were dead. She never said, "Mommy is dead," but she did say, "Mommy's never coming back." She believed herself abandoned, and abandonment in Karen's world was death. She mourned, she was morose for days at a time. Seeing her mother—in whatever condition—might be helpful.

Daniel made sure that he explained what Karen might expect. He told her that her mother would act like a little girl, as if she were playing, only she wasn't playing. She was very confused, and she had forgotten how not to play, but Karen might help her remember. After this talk, Daniel was almost in despair: Who could understand what Will was experiencing, and how could one explain it to a four-year-old? He feared that he would ruin the one good thing to come out of Will's illness: He and Karen had become close; she had dropped her little Miss Humbug personality around him and had given him the gift of her childishness. Just before they went into the room, Daniel crouched down, gave Karen a hug, and looked into her eyes. They were beautifully brown, steady, and unfrightened.

When Will saw Karen, she threw her arms up in front of her chest and head, like a fighter in a protective crouch. Daniel wanted to withdraw, but Karen had already reached Will's bedside. The child evidently thought that her mother was playing a game of peekaboo: She put up a web of fingers in front of her face—half of her digits protruding from the cast she still wore—and she glanced out from behind the screen, now from the right side, now from the left.

Daniel could see Will's taut neck muscles relax, her jaw settle comfortably. Will began to play the game, too. This continued until Karen grew bored. The child crawled up on the bed and tried to sit in her mother's lap. But Will pushed her away; a playful push. A new game began, a wrestling match with Karen trying to climb into Will's lap and Will pushing her off. Karen became exasperated and started to box, swinging wildly with both arms and occasionally using her cast as a tomahawk. Then, stung by the cast, the metal headboard rang out sharply.

Karen screamed and Will took the child into her arms. At first it was a clumsy embrace, a childish one, arms wrapped around the child in an ill-fitting bear hug. But gradually they shifted positions, so that Karen was finally in Will's lap and Will's arms held Karen securely; incongruously sized children became mother and child, the appropriate icon.

"Mommy, it hurts," Karen said.

"I know, Pigeon. It does hurt. I'm sorry." Will looked up at Daniel. Her eyes glistened, brimmed with inchoate tears. "Thank-you," she said.

Will's recovery was quick enough to be called miraculous, but incomplete: she remained unable to walk. She did not resume therapy sessions with Dr. Melford or any of the other physicians on the hospital's staff. Dr. Melford accused her of hostility, of blaming him for the events associated with her time in therapy.

She did not. Her reasonableness had returned with her adult *persona*—she believed in therapy for certain purposes, but she knew or trusted that her problem was essentially a boundary dispute between her ego and God, and that the negotiations were going on in secret.

Most of her time was spent either in her room—reading the Bible or other religious books by the window which looked out toward the mountains—or in the Day Room. The Day Room was a large hall with standing pillars, where patients were free to congregate. The room contained groupings of chairs and couches around magazine tables, and at one end there was a television set. The ceiling was high and the walls were painted a watery green. There were no windows. The room had the feeling of a locker, a forbidding atmosphere of storage, a place where human beings became objects to be kept.

Will came here only to escape the confines of her room. She often sat in her wheelchair in one corner, with her book open on her lap. She thought about her rebellion, her attempt to commit suicide, her effort to make God accept her on her own terms. That had been a diabolical vision: She had seen God with Satan's eye.

Still, she had seen God clearly and for that reason had seen herself, too. She felt that a great measure of grace had been allotted to her; she had been allowed to visit hell. She was not sure, however, that she had returned, that any substantial transformation had occurred. She compared herself to the Apostle Paul after his revelation on the road to Damascus. She, too, now sat in blindness, waiting for word, for instructions concerning what she must do. Would Ananias appear?

Will mostly kept to herself in the Day Room, though occasionally she did chat with other patients. It was difficult to talk because they, like Will, were preoccupied with their own problems, and Will did not really care to trade neurotic histories. She was, however, aware of the others in the Day Room and kept a mental record of the roll.

She began to notice a young man, not more than twenty-five, who wore a bandage around his head and tapped his foot, snapped his fingers, and bobbed in his chair to his own interior music, keeping and passing the time. The young man noticed Will looking at him, and after their eyes met suspiciously for the first few days, he started to wave in greeting in the mornings. After two weeks, the bandage came off, and when he bent over to pick up a magazine off the floor, Will saw the long scar across the front of his scalp. Will was curious; she wheeled over to talk with him.

He saw her coming and waited calmly, smiling a

tricornered smile. She was bashful and girlish when she said, "My name's Will Sunday. I thought we might talk."

"I still can't talk very well, I'm afraid," he said. His words were difficult to understand; they echoed and diffused, as if they issued from a cave.

"Why not?" Will asked.

He pointed to his head. "Surgery."

"Did you have a tumor?"

"Psychosurgery. I was depressed. But now I'm cured."

"What?"

"Been on Thorazine?"

Will shook her head.

"I was on it for years. Couldn't get off; there would have been damage to the nervous system either way. I decided I'd rather have the lesions done by a surgeon. It's worked!" He began to stutter as he became excited. "It was so d-dark, for so long. I was pinned in-n, hed-dged all around. It was dark, bu-but now I can see. I've come into the l-light. I'm cured, you see. I'm fr-ee."

Will had agonized with the young man through his speech; somehow she had known what he was going to say, had almost prompted him at the last. She saw he was tired and felt suddenly exhausted herself. "Maybe you'd better rest now," Will said. "Let's talk tomorrow. Want to?" He nodded.

She wheeled back to her room, rang the bell for the nurse, and asked if she could see Dr. Melford that afternoon. At two o'clock, he entered her room.

He was smiling in a self-satisfied way, his bulldog face plump and proud. "How are you feeling, Will?" he asked rhetorically. "I've missed you. I'm glad you decided you wanted to talk again."

Will was in too much of a hurry to correct his false impression. "I have a question," she said. "I met a young man in the Day Room. I don't know his name, but he's the one who has had psychosurgery."

"He was sent here to recuperate." Dr. Melford lowered his voice and said, "I don't approve of the whole business. I think it's barbaric."

"The way he talked," Will said, "it was as if he had undergone a religious conversion."

"Did he? That's interesting. You see, it's my theory, and many of my colleagues', that psychosurgery is a kind of faith healing. Surgery patients have usually been through every other form of therapy, some quite unpleasant, and they're desperate. They meet these doctors, who are usually pretty autocratic, imposing authority figures, and they tell them that they can heal them. And it's *surgery*, you see: the doctor must know what he's doing. So they sacrifice themselves to these demigods, and afterwards, when they're coming out of the mental confusion that results from surgery, they do feel themselves to be 'reborn,' if you like."

The terms of the negotiations of the boundary dispute between herself and God suddenly became clear, manifest. Through her illness, as now through the young man, God had been seeking her out. Faith healing: if unwarranted faith in a doctor could have such an effect, what curative power must be available through faith in a covenanting Jehovah.

She remembered her revelation: "Trust Me." She, like the young man, had undergone surgery, the cruel mercy of God's scalpel: She had known the pain of His amputation of her divine pretensions. Now Will seemed to stand at the frontier between the sensate world and God's immanence, the daily world and the holy.

She thought to herself, *I am not my own, I am Yours.* And with these words, she crossed the boundary. She saw nothing, she was in effect blind, but she felt warm, as if she had stepped from a cool room out into the sunlight: She knew the warmth of being known with the perfect knowledge that is Love.

Dr. Melford stood beside her. "Will, what's happened?" he asked. "Are you all right?"

"Fine," she said. "Fine."

The next morning Will awoke about eight o'clock when the nurse came in to check on her. The morning nurse was a short, fat Mexican woman, with a beautifully oval face, who wore her hair back in a bun. Will liked her. Unlike many of the staff, who for all their professionalism could not conceal their disapproval of the psychically weak, this nurse treated Will as if she were recovering from an illness—as if she had suffered and deserved pampering.

The nurse asked Will if she would like the shade up. Will did. She had been hearing bells in the distance, a constant tolling which had not flagged ever since she had awakened. She asked the nurse about it.

"Pentecost, Señora. I have been to church already this morning. Look," said the nurse, turning her face full toward the window, "you can see the bell tower." The nurse paused, then said, "I'll get you breakfast." She left the room.

Without hesitating, Will got out of bed and walked over to the window. She located the bell tower; she could see it clearly at the bottom of the mountains. The mountains wore their early morning mantle of violet and blue. The sinuous folds of the ravines partitioned the range into so many fingers of God. She put her hand to the pane, as if she might reach out and touch them.